Women in Korean Politics

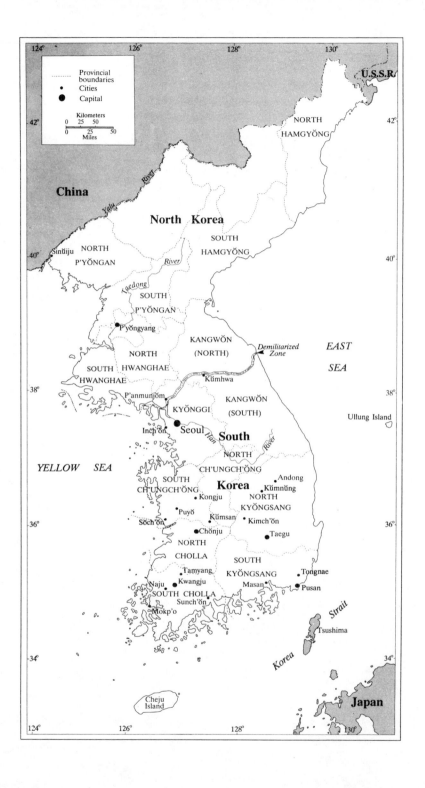

SECOND EDITION

Women in Korean Politics

Chunghee Sarah Soh

Westview Press

BOULDER • SAN FRANCISCO • OXFORD

Published in paperback in 1993 in the United States of America by Westview Press, Inc., 5500 Central Avenue, Boulder, Colorado 80301-2877, and in the United Kingdom by Westview Press, 36 Lonsdale Road, Summertown, Oxford OX2 7EW

The first edition was published in hardcover in 1991 in the United States of America by Praeger Publishers, One Madison Avenue, New York, New York 10010

Library of Congress Cataloging-in-Publication Data
Soh, Chung-Hee
  [Chosen women in Korean politics]
  Women in Korean politics, second edition / Chunghee Sarah Soh.
    p.   cm.
  Originally published: The chosen women in Korean politics. New York : Praeger, 1991.
  Includes bibliographical references and index.
  ISBN 0-8133-2041-0
  1. Women legislators—Korea (South)   2. Women in politics—Korea (South)   3. Korea (South)—Politics and government.   I. Title.
JQ1727.S64   1993
328.5195'073—dc20   93-5956
                                                                              CIP

Printed and bound in the United States of America

The paper used in this publication meets the requirements of the American National Standard for Permanence of Paper for Printed Library Materials Z39.48-1984.

10   9   8   7   6   5   4   3   2

TO

PIONEER WOMEN EVERYWHERE

Contents

Tables and Figures

TABLES

FIGURES

Photographs follow page 76.

Preface to the Second Edition

It is my pleasure and privilege to write a new preface and to acknowledge the support and assistance I received from a number of people to complete the second edition of my book, the original title of which was *The Chosen Women in Korean Politics: An Anthropological Study*. Since its first edition, published by Praeger, appeared in November, 1991, the book has received several reviews in various academic journals, including *American Anthropologist*, *The Journal of Asian Studies*, and *Korea Journal*. I was gratified by positive evaluations it received from my colleagues in the academic community. I am delighted to have Westview Press publish the second edition.

In this paperback edition a partial revision has been carried out to reflect the fast pace of social change in South Korea, particularly in the political arena, in the past several years, and to address the general reader more directly than in the first edition. The introductory and concluding chapters have been rewritten, and other relevant parts in the text, appendix, references, and index have been updated. The use of Korean words, as in the first edition, has been kept at a minimal level. The appendix of biographical notes on seven women legislators (four of whom have the same surname, Kim, without any kin relationships) and a glossary of Korean words used in the text have been retained; the latter will be useful to the nonspecialist reader with no prior knowledge of Korean culture and society.

Since the initial fieldwork in 1985 and 1986, I conducted follow-up studies in the summers of 1990 and of 1992. The details of the initial field research are described in the introductory chapter. My informants for the additional field research included three newly appointed women legislators, three reappointed ones, and two former women ministers as well as an incumbent one in the Office of the Second Minister of the State (which was created in 1988). Although I considered incorporating more material from my follow-up studies into this edition, I chose to limit the revision as indicated above, primarily because the new data would only reconfirm the main thrust of the analysis presented in the previous edition. It can be said safely—but regretfully—that there has been little substantive change in the basic patterns of women's participation in national politics since the 1960s. Nevertheless, it is outside the political structure that we note a significant development in Korean women's political activism in the last few years. A brief discussion of this important aspect of women's political activities is included in the concluding chapter of this new edition.

I want to reaffirm the gratitude I feel toward all the informants who graciously spared their time for in-depth interviewing and placed their trust in me by revealing their life histories and their private thoughts on various issues. Without their cooperation this book would not have been possible. Special thanks are due to Alan Howard, Takie Sugiyama Lebra, and Alice Dewey for their support for my work as my mentors and friends. I gratefully acknowledge the financial support for the fieldwork provided by the National Science Foundation, the East-West Center, and the Association for Asian Studies Committee on Korean Studies.

I also wish to take this opportunity to salute the professional women in the publishing industry I have come to know through my book projects with Praeger Publishers and Westview Press. Taking to heart the proverb "Better late than never," I extend my thanks to Anne Davidson and Talvi Laev at Praeger for their professional competence and courteous assistance to me in preparing the manuscript for the first edition of this book. I am grateful to the members of the editorial board of Westview Press for making this second edition possible. I feel especially indebted to Susan L. McEachern, senior editor at Westview, for her warm support and judicious editorial suggestions to enhance this new edition. Shena Redmond at Westview also deserves my sincere thanks for her careful work in the production process of this book. Finally, I express my heartfelt appreciation to my husband, Jerry D. Boucher, for his support and good humor while I pursued this project against his friendly advice to relax and enjoy the summer.

Chunghee Sarah Soh

Abbreviations

Following are abbreviations used in the text and endnotes:

CCEM   Central Commission for Election Management (Chungang Songgo Kwalli Wiwonhoe)

DP   Democratic Party (Minjudang)

DJP   Democratic Justice Party (Minju Chonguidang)

DRP   Democratic Republican Party (Minju Konghwadang)

EWU   Ewha Women's University (Ewha Yoja Taehakkyo)

KA   *Korea Annual*

KOIS   Korea Overseas Information Service

KWA   Korea Women's Association (Han'guk Puinhoe)

KWDI   Korea Women's Development Institute (Han'guk Yosong Kaebalwon)

KWNP   Korea Women's National Party (Taehan Yoja Kungmindang)

LP   Liberal Party (Chayudang)

NA   National Assembly (Kukhoe)

NCU   National Conference for Unification

NHCC   National History Compilation Committee (Kuksa P'yonch'an Wiwonhoe)

OSMS   Office of the Second Minister of State (Chongmujangkwan che 2 sil)

PCC   Promotion Committee to Commemorate the Sixtieth Birthday of Dr. Yim Yong-sin (Yim Yong-sin Paksa Hoegap Kinyom Saop Ch'ujin Wiwonhoe)

ROK   Republic of Korea

SPC   Sungui Publication Committee (Sungui Ch'ulp'an Wiwonhoe)

NOTE ON ROMANIZATION

Except for those proper names already well known, such as Syngman Rhee, Seoul, and Ewha, and some of the personal names that appear in the acknowledgments and references, the McCune-Reischauer system without its diacritical marks is used for Korean transliteration. In romanizing Korean personal names, the sound changes that may occur between the two syllables of given names are not observed—for example, Kim Ch'ol-an (not Kim Ch'or-an) and Kim Chong-rye (not Kim Chong-nye). When naming persons, in the preface I have followed the American system of placing the given name before the surname. However, in the text I follow the Korean custom of placing the surname before the given name except for such well known names as Syngman Rhee and Helen Kim as well as some authors cited in the references section.

1

Introduction

One of the most remarkable social facts in the present century is that women's roles and status have undergone conspicuous transformations accompanying modernization processes. The expansion of the role of women in public life, particularly in politics, is one of the noteworthy social achievements in this century. At the turn of the century, for example, there was only one country (New Zealand) that granted suffrage to women.[1] By the final quarter of the twentieth century, only a handful of countries, such as Saudi Arabia, legally excluded women from political processes open to men.[2] Since Sirimavo Bandaranaike was elected prime minister of Sri Lanka in 1960,[3] the phenomenon of female chief executives has occurred in several other nations in Asia, Europe, and the Americas.[4] However, except for the Scandinavian countries, with a steadily increasing share of women in national legislatures, most countries show fluctuations in the proportion of women among their legislators.[5]

This book examines the nature and scope of the participation of women in Korean politics at the elite level by studying the life histories of the women members of the National Assembly of the Republic of Korea (ROK, often referred to as South Korea, in contrast to North Korea, whose formal name is the Democratic People's Republic of Korea). Who are these women? How did they attain their political positions? What motivated their participation in male-dominated politics? What meaning do they give to their participation in politics as legislators? What insights would an analysis of their personal and professional experiences provide to our understanding of complex processes of social change? How do the experiences of women in Korean politics compare with those of their counterparts in different nation-states? These are the major questions with which this book is concerned.

The representation of women in national politics at the elite level, I believe, is an important indicator of women's roles and status in society. Only by participating in the central institutions of society (such as the government) on an equal basis can women enhance their social status vis-à-vis men,[6] yet studies show that women are conspicuous by their absence in government and other decision-making positions in the public sphere in most countries and/or cultures.[7] The low participation of women and their underrepresentation in political life may be demonstrated by the minuscule percentage of women in national legislatures, executive cabinets, and chief executive offices across nations,[8] and Korea is no exception.

The membership of the first National Assembly (1948-50) consisted of 199 men and 1 woman. The fourteenth National Assembly, which convened in 1992, has 295 men and 4 women. A total of 46 women found their way into the National Assembly between 1948 and 1992, and 14 of them have served for more than one term (see Table 1.1). Among the 46 women legislators, 5 have also served as cabinet ministers. Although the percentage of females in the Korean labor force grew from 28.6 percent in 1960 to 40.4 percent in 1989,[9] only 0.1 percent of women workers were in administrative and managerial positions.[10] Among the employees of the national government, 23 percent were female in 1988, but women constituted 0.5 percent among the upper ranks of the officials, above the "fifth grade."[11]

Since politics has been traditionally a male occupation, under-representation of females in politics seems a universal fact. Under the circumstances, the question to be asked is not, Why do women not participate in politics? but How and why did these few women become involved in the male bastion of politics at all?

To answer the question concerning the motivations for and processes of the participation of women in national politics, we need to probe into the life histories of women politicians. We must not only learn about their personal backgrounds (such as their family, gender-role socialization, education, religion, and marriage) but also situate the individual variables in the particular cultural background and the sociohistorical circumstances of the country and of the world at the same time. In other words, we have to look for both the individual and the sociocultural factors in order to understand how and why some women entered the political arena.

The goal of this book is twofold: to provide ethnographic materials on the experiences of women in South Korean politics and, more generally, to offer theoretical perspectives on the processes of social change in gender roles and relations. It does not purport to study Korean politics per se. Rather, using gender as an analytical tool,[12] this ethnography of Korean women legislators aims to throw light on various aspects of modern Korean society: the Korean patterns of behavior; the inner workings of the national legislature; the characteristics of the political elite; and the dynamics of changing male-female relations. As a newly industrialized country, South Korea may be referred to as a "patriarchal democracy," for

Table 1.1
The 46 South Korean Women Legislators (1st to 14th National Assembly)

Elected Women Legislators

Name	National Assembly
1. Kim Ch'ol-an**	3, 4
2. **Kim Chong-rye**	11, 12
3. Kim Ok-son	7, 9, 12
4. Kim Yun-dok	(8),* 9, 10
5. **Pak Hyon-suk****	4, (6)*
6. Pak Sun-ch'on**	2, 4, 5, 6, (7)*
7. **Yim Yong-sin****	1, 2

Appointed Women Legislators

1. Chong Pok-hyang, (9)
2. Chu Yang-ja, (14)
3. Han Yang-sun, (12)
4. Ho Mu-in,** (9)
5. **Hwang San-song,** (11)
6. Hyon Ki-sun, (10)
7. Kang Pu-ja, (14)
8. Kang Son-yong, (14)
9. Kim Chang-suk, (12, 13)
10. Kim Haeng-ja,** (10)
11. Kim Hyon-ja, (11, 12)
12. Kim Hyon-suk,** (8)
13. Kim Mo-im, (11)
14. Kim Ok-cha, (8, 9)
15. Kim Ok-yol, (10)
16. Kim Yong-ja, (10)
17. **Kim Yong-jong,** (12)
18. Ku Im-hoe, (9)
19. Mo Yun-suk,** (8)
20. Mun Yong-ju, (11)
21. Pak Chong-ja, (9)
22. Pak Hye-kyong, (12)
23. Pak Hyon-so,** (10)
24. Pak Yong-suk, (13)
25. P'yon Chong-hi, (8)
26. Sin Tong-sun, (10)
27. Sin Yong-sun, (13)
28. So Yong-hi, (9, 10)
29. To Yong-sim, (13)
30. Yang Kyong-ja, (12, 13)
31. Yi Kyong-suk, (11)
32. Yi Mary,** (7)
33. Yi Pom-jun, (9)
34. Yi Suk-chong,** (9)
35. Yi Sung-bok, (9)
36. Yi U-jong, (14)
37. Yi Yong-hi, (11)
38. Yi Yun-ja, (11, 13)
39. Yun Yo-hun, (9, 10)

Note: The names of the five women legislators who also served as cabinet ministers are in bold type.
* Parentheses indicate appointed tenures.
** Deceased as of 1992.

its social structure is characterized by the dual sets of values and beliefs concerning gender roles and relations: one rooted in Korean patriarchal culture preoccupied with the ideology of male superiority, and the other deriving from the Western liberal-democratic principle of sexual equality. What theoretical insights into the dynamics of changing gender roles and relations can we obtain from the experiences of women in Korean politics?[13] This book will consider the question in terms of three specific dimensions of change: (1) social conditions that are conducive to women's entry into politics (Chapter 5); (2) behavioral patterns of male-female interactions (Chapter 7); and (3) private meanings of legislative careers for men and women of this study (Chapter 8).

Scholarly attention on the issues of "women in politics" began in the early 1970s, adding to a burgeoning literature on women and gender inequality. As the first ethnography of professional women in Korean politics, this book will, I hope, contribute to women's studies as well by enriching our general understanding of women in politics cross-culturally. The experiences of Korean women in politics not only delineate the systematic limits to female life in Korean culture. They also reveal cross-national commonalities in social structural impediments to women in high-level public office as well as the empowering impact of the democratic system. In this book I have endeavored to provide cross-cultural comparative perspectives on such topics as family backgrounds, gender-role socialization, the patterns of recruitment, and the impact of the electoral system on the representation of women in national politics.

The common belief that women are uninterested in politics is still very strong. Careful study of the phenomenon of political women in various cultures may debunk some of the myths concerning behavioral differences between the sexes. The apparent paradox of some women receiving high respect and social prestige by trespassing into the "male domain" of politics is intriguing and deserves systematic research. Whether and how their participation in politics may transform the traditional patterns of gender hierarchy in the male-female relations at home and in public, for instance, is an overarching issue of both theoretical and practical import in the study of women in politics.

THE POLITICAL CONTEXT

Defining politics chiefly as the activities of elected and appointed officials in the government, we will explore in the following chapters the details of the particular sociocultural factors affecting the patterns of the participation of women in Korean politics. However, an overview of the political context and women's history in postliberation Korean politics is needed to aid our understanding of the experiences of the women of this study.

The point that needs to be emphasized at the outset about the patterns and processes of political participation of women of this study is that the relationship between women and politics in South Korea is a complex one. It requires a holistic, contextual perspective in order to understand the dynamic interaction among such variables as the personal and professional backgrounds of the individual women (Chapters 3 and 4) and the turbulent history of the sociopolitical climate under the volatile political system of a divided nation groping its way toward a stable, democratic society.

Since liberation from the Japanese in 1945, Korea has gone through a number of major political events and crises, such as the U.S. and Soviet occupation of the peninsula after liberation, the Korean War, the Student Uprising of 1960, the Military Revolution of 1961, and another military coup d'état in 1980. The tumultuous climate of political life in South Korea is well reflected in the several constitutional revisions of the political system, which resulted in six republics during the four decades (see Table 1.2) since the proclamation of the constitution of the Republic of Korea on July 17, 1948. (July 17, Constitution Day, is a national holiday in the ROK.)

At the core of these constitutional revisions were matters concerning the office of the president, such as direct versus indirect election and the conditions of executive office, including presidential tenure.[14] A major consequence of these frequent revisions of the constitution was that the laws concerning the National Assembly and its membership kept changing. During the First Republic (1948-60), for example, the legislature was unicameral. However, the Student Uprising in April, 1960, in protest against the fraudulent election of the president and vice-president the preceding month, ended the First Republic.

The Second Republic began in 1960 with a new constitution that made the National Assembly a bicameral body and the prime minister the chief executive of the administration, thereby reducing the role of president to symbolic head of state. It also decreed the election, instead of the appointment, of the heads of the local governments. The Second Republic, under the leadership of Prime Minister Chang Myon, had to face many difficulties, including political infighting in the ruling Democratic Party, economic distress, and social unrest. Turbulent street demonstrations continued until the spring of 1961, when a military coup d'état took place on May 16.[15] The rationale for the military seizure of government was that civil rule had been a total failure. General Park Chung Hee observed that the Military Revolution was to "suspend democracy temporarily while it is undergoing medical treatment" to create a "miracle on the Han River" by effecting an industrial revolution in Korea.[16] The "Political Purification Law" (Chongchongpop) was promulgated in March, 1962, and a list of

① Syngman Rhee 48-60
② Chang Myon 60-61
③ Park Chung-hee 61-79

Table 1.2
Chronology of the Republic of Korea and the National Assembly

Republic of Korea	National Assembly	
1st Republic (1948-60)	1st NA	(1948-50)
	2nd NA	(1950-54)
	3rd NA	(1954-58)
	4th NA	(1958-60)
2nd Republic (1960-61)	5th NA	(1960-61)
Military Rule (1961-63)		
3rd Republic (1963-72)	6th NA	(1963-67)
	7th NA	(1967-71)
	8th NA	(1971-72)
4th Republic (1972-80)	9th NA	(1973-79)
	10th NA	(1979-80)
5th Republic (1980-88)	11th NA	(1981-85)
	12th NA	(1985-88)
6th Republic (1988-)	13th NA	(1988-92)
	14th NA	(1992-)

Note: NA = National Assembly

Handwritten annotations:

Syngman Rhee

Chang Myon

Park Chung Hee

Yusin

Chun Doo Hwan

Roh Tae Woo

Student Uprising April 1960

Coup May 16/61

71 election against Kim Dae Jung

Park assassinated by Kim Chae Kyu Oct 26, 79

Coup Dec 12, 79

Kwangju May 1980

Roh's June 29 Decl.

4,374 former politicians——whose political activities were to be suspended until the start of the following year——was announced a month later.[17]

A constitutional revision bill approved by a national referendum in December, 1962, changed the National Assembly back to a unicameral body and made the president the chief executive of the administration. Since then, political power has been centralized in the national government, allowing no autonomous local governments. (No local government elections took place until 1991.) Further, the constitution of the Third Republic (1963-72) added the proportional representation system to the method for recruitment of the members of the National Assembly, creating two kinds of legislators: those elected from "regional constituencies" by popular vote and those selected from the "national constituency" by the leadership of political parties.

In 1969, a constitutional amendment was approved by a national referendum to enable President Park to run for the presidency for the third time. Park Chung Hee won the presidential election in 1971 by garnering over six million votes against his opponent, Kim Dae Jung, who received over five million votes. The opposition party declared that the election was rigged, and college students demonstrated, denouncing the election. In October, 1972, the nation was put under martial law, and a constitutional revision bill was announced to "revitalize" the country. A national referendum approved the bill, which included the extension of presidential power to the legislative and judiciary branches of the government, the doubling of presidential tenure to eight years, the elimination of restrictions on the reelection of the president, and the establishment of the National Conference for Unification (NCU). The mission of the NCU was to pursue peaceful unification of the country. In December, 1972, the delegates of the NCU were elected by popular vote, and they in turn elected Park Chung Hee to the office of the president. The new "Revitalizing Reforms" (Yusin) Constitution, was proclaimed and the Fourth Republic (1972-80) began as Park Chung Hee was inaugurated as the eighth president of South Korea on December 27, 1972.[18]

During the Fourth Republic, the National Assembly was composed of the members elected by popular vote and of the members elected by the NCU. All the candidates elected by the NCU had been recommended by President Park. In addition to the slate of recommended candidates, the president also submitted a list of reserve candidates in a fixed order who, upon the approval of the NCU, could take over the vacated memberships in the National Assembly.[19] The legislators elected by the NCU made up one-third of the legislative membership and belonged to the Yujonghoe (Society for the Revitalizing Reforms Politics).[20] The tenure of the legislators elected by popular vote was six years, whereas those elected by the NCU had a three-year tenure.

The proportional representation party list system was retained in the constitutions of both the Fifth and the Sixth Republics "to encourage leading technocrats" to participate in legislative life and "to revitalize democratic party policies."[21] Thus, four-fifths of the members of the fourteenth National Assembly were elected by popular vote, whereas the remaining one-fifth of the total legislative seats were distributed proportionately among political parties that had won five seats or more in the direct election.[22]

In this study, for purposes of comparison, members of the former group are referred to as "elected legislators" and those of the latter group as "appointed legislators." Appointed legislators are often perceived in a negative light by the public, owing to the indirect method of their election by the party leadership.[23] It is important to underline here the implications of the two categories of women legislators for the basic differences in their attitudes toward and skills for political careers. The majority of the appointed women legislators may be regarded as passive political appointees. In contrast, all elected women legislators and several appointed women legislators (mostly partisans) belong to the category of "political women"—women who possess the desire and necessary skills to seek positions of jural authority, wield significant influence in the decision-making processes of public life, and *actively seek* continued participation in power processes.[24]

In addition to the mode of recruitment, motivational differences among women legislators further separate them into pioneer- and second-generation legislators: those who became legislators before the "May Sixteenth Military Revolution" of 1961,[25] and those who became legislators after it. Women legislators of the pioneer generation began their political involvement under Japanese rule, with the March First Independence Movement of 1919 (see Chapter 5), and continued their political participation in postliberation Korea. Women legislators of the second generation—except for three—are appointed members of the National Assembly, and the majority of them did not voluntarily seek active political participation. In most cases political socialization followed their appointments to the legislature. For the three elected women legislators of the second generation, intense personal experiences of major political events after liberation motivated their lifelong commitment to political careers.

The nation was placed under martial law once again after President Park was assassinated by Kim Chae-kyu, the director of the Korean Central Intelligence Agency, on October 26, 1979. General Chun Doo Hwan led a lightning coup on December 12, 1979, and arrested a number of key military figures implicated in Park's death.[26] Within six months a new group of military elite under the leadership of General Chun took power, after violent quelling of the street demonstrations in Kwangju in May, 1980. (The bloody confrontation that occurred between the military and the citizens of Kwangju in May, 1980, has been variously referred to as the Kwangju "incident," the Kwangju "affair," the Kwangju "uprising," or the Kwangju "democratization movement," reflecting divergent perspectives of the event and changes in political climate over the years.[27] The anti-American sentiment among the radical students and political activists,[28] which emerged in the 1980s, has much to do with their perception of the tacit U.S. support of the military action during the Kwangju uprising and of the subsequent Chun regime.)[29]

In August, 1980, General Chun Doo Hwan was elected president by the National Conference for Unification. The Fifth Republic began when a new constitution approved by a national referendum took effect on October 27, 1980; it automatically disbanded the National Assembly and political parties. On the following day, President Chun appointed eighty-one people (including Kim Chong-rye, the only second-generation elected woman legislator endorsed by the ruling party) to the Legislative Council for National Safeguarding (Kukka powi ippop hoeui), which functioned as the national legislature until the eleventh National Assembly convened in April, 1981.

New political parties were formed in January, 1981, and the Democratic Justice Party (DJP) nominated Chun Doo Hwan as its presidential candidate. Chun Doo Hwan was elected president by the presidential electoral college in February, 1981. The issue of political legitimacy plagued the Chun administration throughout his seven-year tenure. When President Chun anointed Roh Tae Woo—another former military general—as the presidential candidate of the ruling DJP on June 10, 1987, the antipathy toward the Chun regime exploded, with violent street demonstrations staged by college students in Seoul. A wave of fierce protest demonstrations quickly spread to other major cities, where students fighting with rocks and homemade gasoline bombs were bombarded with tear gas by the riot police. Finally, the stunning announcement of the "June 29 declaration" by then-candidate Roh helped to resolve the crisis. Roh's declaration appeased the general public and the opposition alike with a list of reform measures, which included an endorsement of direct presidential elections and other major sociopolitical reforms. The constitution was revised again before the Sixth Republic, under the leadership of President Roh Tae Woo, who was elected directly by popular vote, began in 1988. The political climate has been steadily improving, moving toward liberal democracy. In 1993 Kim Yong Sam became the first civilian chief executive since the 1961 military coup, and he initiated major reform actions to forge a "New Korea."

It should be noted here that women's grass-roots political activism, which regressed after the Korean War and throughout the 1960s, began to reemerge in the 1970s and expanded significantly under the impact of the U.N. Decade for Women (1975-85) and the general trend toward liberalization in the 1980s ROK politics. Although an in-depth analysis of women's participation in grass-roots political activism is beyond the scope of this book, we will consider one aspect of the phenomenon in the concluding chapter.

STUDYING WOMEN LEGISLATORS

When my research on women in Korean politics began in 1985—following the election of the twelfth National Assembly (1985-88)—thirty-nine women had served in the National Assembly, and eight of them were deceased. Of the thirty-one former or incumbent members of the National Assembly who were alive, twenty-six agreed to meet with me for an interview. I was unable to interview the remaining five women (who were all appointed legislators) for the following reasons: Two declined my request on the grounds of illness; the third, who had resigned from her legislative post shortly after her appointment to the twelfth National Assembly, refused to be interviewed; the fourth woman avoided being interviewed by repeatedly postponing our meeting; and the address of the fifth woman was unavailable.

The total number of either former or incumbent women legislators interviewed for this study came to twenty-six. I used a detailed interview schedule that had three parts: private life, public life, and a section on values and opinions. The aim of these in-depth, semistructured interviews was to collect as much information as possible on the life histories of the sample for a holistic understanding of women's involvement in Korean politics. As to those women who were not available for interviews, I obtained basic information on their personal and professional backgrounds through official documents and records. I also interviewed relatives and friends of both living and deceased elected women legislators to collect supplementary data. In addition, I interviewed some male informants, including two leading legislators of the ruling Democratic Justice Party and consulted historical documents to complement these firsthand data.[30] Scholarly publications on Korean culture and sociopolitical history constituted important supplementary data for this research.

The main sample of this study consists of twenty-nine women legislators: twenty-two appointed and all seven elected ones. Three of the seven elected women legislators were deceased at the time this study began, but substantial biographical materials on them exist. I selected fourteen women out of the sample for intensive study on the basis of their length of service in the legislature. They constitute the core of the sample: the seven elected lawmakers and the seven appointed ones who served more than one term.

There are two categories of life history data on which this book is based: (1) life histories that were elicited directly from the informants during the interviews and (2) various published materials on female legislators drawn from newspapers, magazines, pamphlets, government documents, biographies, and autobiographies. The first category, life histories, was systematically collected for the purpose of understanding the issues of gender inequality in political participation. The second category provided information on the assemblywomen who are no longer living.

In using the second category of life history data, however, we have to be mindful that the items were written for diverse purposes by various writers: Magazine and newspaper articles were written by journalists to provide information on female lawmakers to the general public, while books were written by friends and admirers to laud the accomplishments of the pioneer generation of political women. Political campaign literature, of course, presents profiles of the candidates in a favorable light for the purpose of winning an election. A few former women legislators wrote autobiographies to reflect on their personal lives as female politicians or to set the record straight concerning some aspects of their professional and private lives.

Although life histories are the unique stories of each individual, they are also products of a particular culture in a particular period of its history. This convergence of biographical and ethnological elements permits us to treat life histories as a source of valuable data to generate hypotheses concerning human behavior. However, because life histories are remembered and consequently subjective accounts of individual lives, some social scientists have been uneasy about their use.[31] Also, anthropologists' concern for their informants' being representative of their culture has meant that until recently ethnology has tended to shy away from the study of extraordinary individuals.[32] Nevertheless, the study of extraordinary individuals is important if we want to learn the ways people manage to weave into their lives "the patterns of personal leeway and freedom" in spite of the various constraints imposed by their society and culture.[33] It allows us to explore the effects of sociocultural constraints in personal lives and to portray the ways in which people manipulate and influence their culture.[34]

Life histories also allow us the advantage of hindsight in sorting out events and experiences that served as "turning points" in the lives of political women.[35] Only the life history method can achieve this. For this study, it can glean from personal histories some insights into the conditions that are conducive to the political participation of women and into the processes of women's involvement in politics, as will be discussed in detail in Chapter 5. Therefore, despite the many problems of subjectivity and interpretation that are involved in the use of life histories, we can profitably use them to study social change, as clues to implicit themes, as documentation of roles, as demonstration of socialization and enculturation, and as an entry into understanding personality.[36] Life history as a subjective report furnishes us with the insider's point of view, and in our study of the issues of gender and political participation, it is essential to systematically gather the subjective viewpoints of female politicians on these issues.

In this book, I present as much as possible the insiders' views by directly quoting what my informants related to me concerning their lives as women in politics. Also, more attention is given to elected women legislators than appointed ones because the former represent women who actively sought political careers, and because the personal data obtained for the elected women legislators were relatively more detailed, fascinating, and dramatically illustrative of the challenges women face in seeking political positions than the data gathered from the appointed ones. Nevertheless, whenever possible, I take a comparative perspective, contrasting the data on elected legislators with the data on appointed ones, and among the elected, I highlight the generational differences between pioneer- and second-generation women lawmakers.

Protecting the privacy of the informants is a serious responsibility of the researcher, particularly when the life history approach is used with informants who are highly educated career women in a literate society. Therefore, in my quotations, I have tried to preserve the anonymity of my informants, especially the appointed women legislators, but I revealed their names when the subject did not seem to warrant concern for privacy.

NOTES

1. Newland (1975); Pharr (1981).
2. Randall (1987).
3. For a biography of Sirimavo Bandaranaike, see Seneviratne (1975).
4. For profiles of several women chief executives, see Bennett (1986).
5. Newland (1975); Pharr (1981); Randall (1987).
6. Schlegel (1977).
7. Quinn (1977).
8. Randall (1987); Sivard (1985).
9. Korea Women's Development Institute (KWDI) (1985:512, 1991:137).
10. KWDI (1991:144).

11. Nine "grades" and two research positions comprise the eleven ranks for government employees in the general service category; the first grade is at the top, while the positions of researcher and assistant researcher are listed at the bottom of the hierarchy (KWDI 1985:529, 1991:220).

12. Gender in this study is defined as cultural constructions of sex-appropriate temperament, social roles, and relations for males and females, which, of course, derive from biological differences between the sexes but vary cross-culturally. For a discussion of gender as an analytic category, see Scott (1986).

13. For an detailed discussion of the question, see Soh (1993a).

14. For more details on the constitutional revisions, see K.-b. Kim (1974a, 1974b), Korea Overseas Information Service (KOIS) (1987), and M. Yi (1985). For a concise description in English of the political history of South Korea (1948-90), see Eckert et al. (1990:347-88).

15. For a comprehensive analysis of the demise of the Second Republic, see Han (1974). Also, see Gosfield and Hurwood (1969) and Oh (1975) for detailed descriptions of the sociopolitical situation during the Second Republic.

16. Lovell (1975:176-79).

17. *Dong-a Yon'gam* (1985:41).

18. On motivational factors for the Yusin reforms, see Cumings (1984:43-44); Han (1984:264-66); and Park (1979). For the text of the Yusin Constitution in English, see Wright (1975).

19. Article 40 of the Yusin Constitution.

20. Yujonghoe is a contracted form of Yusin-jonguhoe (Society of Political Friends for Revitalizing Reforms).

21. See KOIS (1987:267).

22. See Tables 5.1 and 5.2 for details on the varying ratios of appointed to elected legislators since the sixth National Assembly.

23. Darcy and Song (1986:683) state that the attitudes developed during the Park regime toward the members of the Yujonghoe carried over to the subsequent National Assembly, despite "a very different basis" of the election under President Chun. However, it should be pointed out that since both Presidents Park and Chun, as the top decision makers, fully exercised their authority in recruiting the legislative members at large, the "different basis" of their recruitment under President Chun was more formal than substantive. For further discussions of the negative perceptions of the PR system by the general public, see Chapters 6 and 7.

24. For an extended definition of "political women," see Kirkpatrick (1974:217-18).

25. Koreans often use dates in naming sociohistorical and political events, such as Samil (Three-One, i.e., the March First) movement, Yuk'io (Six-Two-Five, i.e., the June Twenty-Fifth) war, and Oilyuk (Five-One-Six,

i.e., the May Sixteenth) military revolution.

26. For a brief description in English of the political scenes surrounding the assassination and its aftermath, see Scalapino (1981:144-46).

27. See Clark (1988) for a collection of papers on the Kwangju issue.

28. For a detailed discussion in English of anti-Americanism in South Korea, see Clark (1991).

29. The healing of both the physical and the emotional wounds suffered by the residents of Kwangju since 1980 remains a major sensitive task of the new administration under President Kim.

30. For more details of methodology, see Soh (1987/1988).

31. For a concise review of developments in the "Anthropology of Life Stories," see Kendall (1988:11-15).

32. Clifford (1978).

33. Clifford (1978:53).

34. Sheridan and Salaff (1984:1).

35. See Mandelbaum (1973) for a discussion of "turning point" as an analytical concept for the study of life histories.

36. Kluckhohn (1945).

2

A Cultural Account

A major assumption of this study is that while personality traits are important, sociohistorical forces are ultimately responsible for female participation in politics. Sociocultural factors (such as the sexual division of labor into the public/male and domestic/female spheres, the influence of family structure on feminine personality, and the ideology of male superiority) effectively constrain women from developing their human potential as independent, able social beings in the public sphere.[1] Across nations, women as a group are less educated than men and are engaged in lower-paying and less prestigious jobs than their menfolk.[2] The gender gap in political life, for instance, is a direct consequence of the traditional gender-role system, which has restricted women to the domestic sphere.

"WIDOW'S SUCCESSION"

A notable finding about women legislators in South Korea is that none of them attained their political position by assuming their deceased husbands' posts. In contrast, conjugal ties and "widow's succession" have provided legitimate channels to political office for women in many other industrialized nations and tribal societies.

For example, the world's first woman prime minister, Sirimavo Bandaranaike, assumed office as the widow of the slain Sri Lankan political leader Solomon Bandaranaike. In the tribal societies of the Mende and Sherbro of Sierra Leone, one of the traditional means by which a woman would become head of her chiefdom was to succeed to high office as the chief's wife upon her husband's death.[3] In the United States, three of the ten female senators between 1917 and 1964 obtained their seats by appointment to fill the vacancies caused by the deaths of their husbands, and most women in the United States Congress until 1949 had won their seats in Congress via "widow's succession."[4] In recent years, Corazon Aquino, the first woman president of the Philippines, also entered the political arena after the assassination of her politician husband.

Even in Japan, where male-female relations have traditionally been based on the same Confucian ideology of male superiority as in Korea, many women who achieved political note were either from political families or were "political widows" who served their husbands' constituencies after their deaths.[5] Some women went into politics on behalf of their "purged" men (e.g., husbands or brothers whose political careers were suspended for their wartime crimes) in the first postwar general election.[6] In France, too, the widows of wartime resistance heroes were elected to the Assembly.[7]

It is surprising, therefore, that not a single female legislator in South Korea achieved her position by dint of being a "political widow." Another difference between Korean assemblywomen and the women politicians of other countries such as Japan, Sri Lanka, the Philippines, Europe, and the United States is that Korean women legislators—with the exception of one woman who grew up and married in the United States—used their maiden names regardless of their marital status. Why? What does this tell us about Korean culture and society?

The absence of widow's succession to political positions of their deceased husbands in Korean political history reflects at least two aspects of the traditional Korean social structure.[8]

First of all, it is a manifestation of the legacy of the traditional social structure that stresses the paramount importance of male bloodlines. It is well illustrated in adoption practices that emphasize the purity of the patrilineal bloodline. Adoption for Korean couples in the late Yi dynasty (1392-1910) meant taking "the son of a brother or cousin" of the husband to succeed to the family headship.[9] In modern Korea, the custom is reinforced by the civil code that denies "an adopted child whose surname and clan origins are not common with those of his adoptive father" the right to succeed to the family headship of the adoptive family.[10]

In a society like Korea, which is organized on strictly patrilineal principles, a wife is an "associate member" of her husband's lineage (*munjung*). She has to fulfill her duties as a daughter-in-law, wife, and mother before she can finally achieve the status of an ancestor in her husband's clan upon her death.[11] Women retain the surnames of their natal families throughout their lives, and that is why Korean female legislators use their maiden names regardless of their marital status. This custom symbolizes the wife's separateness from the husband's lineage in the Korean family structure and should not be interpreted as evidence of sexual equality practiced in the Korean tradition. It manifests the value that Koreans place on the purity of the patrilineal bloodline. In the strictly patrilineal Korean society, with its deep-rooted bias for the male bloodline, it has been unthinkable for a wife to succeed to the office of her husband.

Therefore, so long as the patrilineal principles of the social structure retain their traditional strength, it is unlikely that Korean politics will witness a "political widow" who assumes the post of her deceased politician husband.

Secondly, the nonexistence of "political widows" in Korean politics underscores the rigidity with which gender-role division has been maintained in Korean society. Gender-role division was symbolized by the spatial segregation of the sexes at home in the traditional architecture. The *yangban* upper-class house in the Yi dynasty, for example, was divided into male quarters and female quarters.[12] And the separation of male/public and female/domestic roles was scrupulously upheld. The public sphere belonged to men. The exceptions officially made for the women of the Yi dynasty were the four professional service roles of the shaman, palace woman, female physician, and courtesan.[13] The lives of the *yangban* upper-class women were more strictly confined to the private, domestic sphere than were those of lower-class women, who were often forced to work outside the home for economic reasons. There existed no honorable, prestigious roles for women in the public sphere. Hence, one may assert that the prestige and social status of a Yi woman was inversely related to her social power in the public domain.[14]

Even though the Yi dynasty ended in 1910, its cultural legacy remains very strong. Politics is still an eminently male domain, and the notion of a "political widow" is unthinkable for most Koreans, whose gender-role attitudes are steeped in patrilineal rules and Confucian values. As is discussed later in this chapter, the contradictions between the democratic and Confucian gender-role ideologies constitute a major ethnographic context in which the life histories of women legislators of this book should be viewed.

QUEENS AND QUEEN MOTHERS

Historically, it was only during the Silla dynasty (57 B.C.-935 A.D.) that the Korean people had female heads of state. The appearance of these queens was due to the "bone-rank" (*kolp'um*) institution, a unique status system that regulated a variety of special privileges according to hereditary bloodline.   The bone-rank system of the royal clan was further distinguished into the "sacred-bone" (*songgol*) and "true-bone" (*chin'gol*) ranks. These nobles held the top five of seventeen government positions, and royal succession until Queen Chindok (the twenty-eighth monarch) was limited to the sacred-bone rank, which included not only the king's sons but also daughters, brothers, and sons-in-law.[15]   Thus, in the hierarchical society of the Silla kingdom, women were able to succeed to the throne in the absence of qualified male heirs.

Queen Sondok, the twenty-seventh monarch, who reigned for fifteen years from 632 to 647, was the first woman to occupy the throne of Silla because the male line of the sacred-bone rank had died out. Her successor was also a woman: her cousin, Queen Chindok, reigned for seven years until 654. The two queens sagaciously ruled Silla at a critical time when the conflict between the three kingdoms which constituted the Korean peninsula—Koguryo (37 B.C.-668 A.D.), Paekche (18 B.C.-660 A.D.), and Silla (57 B.C.-935 A.D.)—was at its height.[16] Queen Chindok was succeeded by King Muyol (r. 654-661), who came from the true-bone rank.

After Silla unified the three kingdoms in 668, it had one more female ruler. Queen Chinsong (the fifty-first monarch)—who ruled for ten years (887-897)—came to the throne after King Chonggang (r. 886-887) died without heirs. Pointing to the examples provided by the two previous queens, he had recommended his sister, Chinsong, as his successor. When Queen Chinsong came to the throne, the Silla dynasty was already in decline. She failed to pull the country together and was criticized for misrule and promiscuous personal conduct.[17] Feeling responsible for social unrest, she abdicated from the throne in the tenth year of her reign. She appointed her fifteen-year-old nephew, Hyo, to succeed to the throne. When she found Hyo (who was reputed to be an illegitimate son of her deceased brother, King Chonggang) in the ninth year of her reign, the queen reportedly confirmed Hyo to be the son of her deceased brother, since the boy shared a special characteristic of the "backbone structure of her family."[18]

The bone-rank system disappeared with the demise of the Silla dynasty, but the reference to the bone as a symbolic marker of social status can still be found in the figurative speech of modern Koreans. For example, a person from a reputable family is referred to as a person from *ppyodae innun chiban* (literally, a family with a bone structure) and a man with a bone structure of classic good looks may be admired for his *kwigol* (literally, aristocratic bone), particularly by physiognomists, who will forecast a good fortune for their *kwigol* customers.

Aside from the three queens of Silla, a few other royal women were able to participate in national politics with legitimate political authority. Three of the five instances of regency in the three kingdoms, for instance, were by queen mothers. In the Koryo dynasty (918-1392) some queen consorts also served as regents.[19] The first woman regent in the Koryo dynasty was the Queen Dowager Honae, one of the wives of King Kyongjong (r. 975-981). Her regency started when her eighteen-year-old son Mokchong (r. 997-1009) succeeded to the throne in 997, and ended when the king was deposed in 1009 by Kang Cho, the military commander of the northwest frontier region.[20] During her regency the queen mother had given birth to a son fathered by Kim Ch'i-yang, both of whom were eliminated during the military coup d'état by Kang Cho.[21]

In the Yi dynasty (1392-1910), several queens were able to enter the political arena, despite the strict social-structural exclusion of women from the extradomestic sphere. The queens wielded a great deal of political power, especially in their roles as mothers of the ruling monarchs. Queen Min (r. 1866-1895), who may be regarded as "the ablest female politician in the history of the dynasty,"[22] was an exception in that she played a major political role as the wife of King Kojong (r. 1864-1907) in the latter half of the nineteenth century.

The first woman to become a regent in the Yi dynasty was Queen Yun, the wife of King Sejo (r. 1455-68), who played a decisive role in the selection of her second son—in place of her first grandson—as heir to the throne. Then, as the mother of the nineteen-year-old monarch, Yejong (r. 1468-69), she became regent and initiated her regency in 1468. When Yejong died a year after his succession to the throne, the queen mother selected her thirteen-year-old second grandson Songjong (r. 1469-1494) to succeed to the throne. She then continued her regency for seven more years until 1476.[23]

Although extenuating circumstances allowed the queen mother to step over the boundary of gender-role spheres, Confucian rules of behavior, which stipulate separation of the sexes from the age of seven, had to be observed. The dilemma was handled by the decorous placement of a curtain between the queen mother (who usually sat beside the minor king) and male members of the court when they met to discuss state affairs. This is why the regency by a Queen Mother is referred to as *suryom ch'ongjong*, "administering state affairs from behind a curtain."

The institution of *suryom ch'ongjong* (or regency by the queen mother) underscores the high cultural premium encompassing the maternal role of a married woman who produced male offsprings. Hence, even though the social structure of the Yi dynasty prevented women from participating in extradomestic life, some women participated in national politics and ruled the country as mothers of minor kings. The case of Queen Mother Yun illustrates the point. She became the de facto ruler after the death of her husband, King Sejo. However, widow's succession under the patrilineal principle was structurally impossible. Instead, her participation in the political decision-making process was organized as an interim affair to fulfill her maternal role[24]—which is perhaps the most highly valued role of women, even in contemporary Korea. The regency of Queen Yun (or Chonghi Taebi, as she was referred to in her role of queen mother)[25] was based on the recognition of her maternal role to aid her minor son, who was the legitimate heir to the throne. What needs to be emphasized here is that the key to her formal political participation lay in being the *mother* of a young monarch (Yejong), not the *wife* of a deceased ruler (Sejo).[26]

Her regency was not a case of "widow's succession" but the custodial right of a queen mother. Dynastic lineage charts in a recent history book by a respected scholar underscore this point by omitting the names of dowager-regents.[27] Women as dowager-regents may have been de facto rulers but had not succeeded to the throne.

The rule of royal succession in the Yi dynasty was never explicitly codified. The ruling monarch had absolute discretion in selecting his successor. When a king died without heirs or a will, however, it was left to the queen dowager to choose a successor, as did Queen Mother Yun in choosing King Songjong (r. 1469-1494), as described above. The power of royal women as queens—except Queen Min (r. 1866-1895)—was negligible, but their power as queen mothers or eldest dowagers during regencies was supreme. As the first female regent of the Yi dynasty, Queen Mother Yun set off the pattern of royal women's political participation and power. Two women became regents in the sixteenth century.[28] In the nineteenth century there were four instances of regency by a queen dowager.[29]

SEXUAL EQUALITY AND MALE SUPERIORITY

In Korea, where women's lives were once traditionally confined within the walls of their houses, modernization has provided unprecedented opportunities for women to participate in the public sphere. The introduction of democratic ideology and other Western values has led to constitutional acknowledgment of sexual equality and provided a range of options in women's roles in the public sphere in modern Korea. Article 10 of the constitution stipulates: "All citizens shall be equal before the law, and there shall be no discrimination in political, economic, civic or cultural life on account of sex, religion or social status."[30]

However, the norms and values that guide gender relations in daily life continue to be based on the Confucian ideology of male superiority. The concept of sexual equality is fundamentally alien to the Confucian world view, which regards society as an "ordered inequality."[31] The Koreanization of Confucian teachings further stressed inherited social status and roles—determined permanently at birth—over individual will and freedom of choice.[32]

Hence, although the social structure of South Korea, as embodied in the constitution, enables a woman to run for the presidency in public life, she is still ineligible to become the household head in domestic life, except temporarily. On the surface, the laws concerning family life emphasize sexual equality and give women rights to control their personal property and to marry without parental consent if they are of age. However, these rights are counterbalanced by older patriarchal notions, such as that sons, rather than daughters or wives, are to succeed to the household headship. The old Family Law—which went into effect in 1960 and was revised in 1977—upheld the patriarchal values in such matters as the family headship, boundaries of relatives, adoption, and property and parental custody rights in cases of divorce.[33] After more than a decade's campaign by the leaders of women's organizations, a bill proposing a major revision of the Family Law was finally passed in 1989. However, the new Family Law maintains the system of family headship and still favors sons over daughters in the role of the family headship.[34] The sexual equality in marriage and family life endorsed by the Article 34 of the constitution is thus compromised in the Family Law in order to preserve Korea's "beautiful and good customs" (*mip'ung yangsok*).[35] Thus, the interplay between the dual gender role ideologies, one based on the modern democratic principle of sexual equality and the other on the traditional Confucian attitude of male superiority, complicates the patterns and processes of social change in the area of gender role performance.

The structural duality of modern Korean society has received serious scholarly attention of late.[36] Vincent Brandt, for example, noted two separate systems of ideas and behavior operating in village social organizations: one that is based on lineage-centered, restrained, and hierarchical orientation and the other that is rooted in community-based, spontaneous, and egalitarian outlook.[37] The contradictory themes in Korean life are cultural legacies of the Yi dynasty (1392-1910), a highly stratified society that distinguished upper-class culture from that of the commoners by various material, legal, and symbolic means.[38] Biaxial structures or contrasted opposites, however, may be found in any culture.[39] What is noteworthy about Korean cultural tradition is that the contrasted opposites in these dichotomous sets—the male versus female, or urban versus folk cultures, or the great versus little traditions—were invariably perceived in hierarchical relationships. For instance, a clear demarcation between male and female domains was maintained, and things that belonged to the female domain were devalued, while those that belonged to the male domain were highly valued. And the strict division of labor into male/public and female/domestic spheres in the Yi dynasty meant that women could not take part in public life. Only men participated in it and could aspire to become scholar-officials to bring honor and wealth to the family.

Even though modernization processes have affected the old social structure in various aspects, the cultural legacy of the Yi dynasty continues to influence male-female relations in modern Korean society. Korea reportedly is "one of the three countries in the world with the highest boy-preference attitude," the other two being India and Taiwan.[40] The official adoption of Western democratic idealism, which is in many ways fundamentally opposed to the old value system, has generated confusion and complexities in the social life of contemporary Korea.[41]

The contradictions between the democratic and Confucian ideologies concerning gender roles, for example, were manifest in the campaign experiences of women legislators. Whether a woman candidate ran in the rural towns in 1948—as did Kim Ch'ol-an (see Chapter 5)—or in the capital city of Seoul in the 1980s, she had to defend and justify the pursuit of a political career as a woman. Kim Chong-rye, who ran for a legislative seat at a district in Seoul in 1981, stated during the interview that at first men in the district office of her party as well as some residents of the district had complained that their candidate was not only an outsider but a woman, saying that "A skirt is a skirt. . . . Why should we have a skirt?"[42]

Given these social realities, a fundamental question that needs to be addressed in this book is: How does a society whose social order is based on Confucian patriarchy come to terms with the democratic ideology of sexual equality? Adaptive strategies employed by women legislators (described in Chapter 7) offer some insights into the ways Koreans cope with the contradictions generated by the dual gender role ideologies of their society.

NOTES

1. For example, see Chodorow (1974), Ortner (1974), and Rosaldo (1974).

2. See Sivard (1985) for a statistical summary of women's status throughout the world.

3. Hoffer (1972).

4. Werner (1966:24).

5. Pharr (1977).

6. Jones (1975:717).

7. Vallance (1979).

8. The term "social structure" has been given various definitions by different theorists (see Radcliffe-Brown [1940], Leach [1954], Levi-Strauss [1969]). My own view in this study is closer to Leach's in that social structure here refers to "a set of rules which govern social relations."

9. Peterson (1983:34).

10. Article 877-2, as quoted in H. Lee (1980).

11. Janelli and Janelli (1982).

12. The term *yangban* refers to the civil and military officials in the Koryo (918-1392) and the Yi (1392-1910) dynasties. It subsequently came

to designate the status group in Yi dynasty society (Henderson 1968:17; K. Lee 1984:173-75). It has been variously translated as the gentry, the landowner-scholar-official class (Chung 1982), the literati, the nobility, the ruling class (Y. Kim 1979:47), the members of the two orders of officialdom (K. Lee 1984), and the upper class.

13. Harvey (1979:3).

14. Koh (1975).

15. For more details on the *kolp'um*, see P. Kim et al. (1983), Y. Kim (1979:36-39), and K. Lee (1984:49-50).

16. For more details, see P. Kim et al. (1983:89-97).

17. Y. Kim (1979:28). For a more sympathetic, feminist evaluation of her "misrule," see Pang (1980:154-56).

18. For more details, see P. Kim et al. (1983:227-28).

19. Y. Kim (1979:29-30).

20. K. Lee (1984:126).

21. Pang (1980:199-201).

22. Palais (1975:45).

23. Pang (1980:305-14).

24. For a discussion of the structural versus organizational approaches to the analysis of social action, see Firth (1954).

25. Y. Kim (1979:114).

26. This traditional precedence of maternal role over wifely role continues to influence the behavior of many Korean women today in their marital lives.

27. K. Lee (1984:387-94).

28. Y. Kim (1979:115-16).

29. Palais (1975).

30. Korea Overseas Information Service (KOIS) (1980:10).

31. Bodde (1953:48). For a discussion of Confucian tradition in modern Korea, see Chung (1982).

32. For a discussion of ramifications of the opposing value structures in Korean politics, see Hahm (1975).

33. Family law is contained in Articles 4 and 5 of the Korean Civil Code. For a further discussion of the compromising nature of the old Family Law, see Jacobs (1985:214-15) and Strawn (1981).

34. Office of the Second Minister of State (OSMS)(1990).

35. Article 34 states: "Marriage and family life shall be entered into and sustained on the basis of individual dignity and equality of the sexes" (KOIS 1980:16).

36. See, for instance, Brandt (1971), Dix (1980), H. Lee (1980), and McBrian (1977).

37. Brandt (1971).

38. Y. Kim (1979); Osgood (1951).

39. McCann (1983:134).

40. Cha, Chung, and Lee (1977:113).

41. See H. Lee (1980) for a discussion of the dual marriage system as an illustration of the institutional contradictions in modern Korea.

42. According to Kim Chong-rye, many of them changed their attitudes once they heard her speech at a joint meeting of the candidates.

3

Family Backgrounds and Education

The fundamental importance of family background in the political socialization of women has been noted in various studies conducted in developed countries on the issues of gender and political participation.[1] For example, the majority of female state legislators in the United States had politically active parents.[2] Many Norwegian women politicians also had parents or husbands holding party membership and party or public office.[3]

Among the Korean women legislators of this study, however, none of the elected women legislators had parents or husbands who held political positions or party memberships. Only a few appointed legislators had politically active fathers or husbands; one had a father who had been a prominent member of the National Assembly. Another appointed woman lawmaker stated that her father had been a high official in a local government. Two other appointed women legislators had husbands who had served as high government officials, under Presidents Rhee and Park, respectively. This contrast in the family background between the elected and appointed women legislators is a subtle reflection of some fundamental differences between the two groups of women legislators, with regard to their personal backgrounds and the processes of their political participation. Chapters 3 through 6 present the details of these differences.

PARENTAL FAMILY

Because the parental family is the first social institution a person belongs to and the one he or she grows up in, parental influence on the gender-role orientation of a child is most profound and significant. A study of female political volunteers in Japan, for instance, reported that they came from families where parents permitted their daughters a wide range of latitude for personal growth and adult role experimentation.[4] A recent study on U.S. women reported that the most active political participants tended to be women whose *fathers* were professionals.[5] American women executives and Japanese professional women in male-dominant careers also experienced the positive influence of their fathers on their occupational achievements.[6] Other researchers have also found fathers' interactions with children to be of greatest interest in the social psychological development of children.[7] Some have suggested that perhaps the characteristics of the father are even more important than those of the mother in determining children's attitudes.[8]

Fathers and Daughters

Although the incidence of politically active parents or husbands was extremely low in the case of women legislators of this study, the nature of relationships between them and their parents, especially their fathers, seemed of particular significance in the personal and professional developments of both elected and appointed women legislators. However, there was a stark opposition in the nature of the father-daughter relationship between the two groups.

The life histories of the *elected* women legislators of this study suggested that the paternal contribution to political careers of the daughters was made by *absent fathers*, while many *appointed* women legislators attributed their professional successes to their *supportive fathers*. The contrastive patterns of paternal influence in the lives of the elected versus appointed women legislators, as is discussed below, are reflections of the particular sociohistorical circumstances under which they grew up and the different occupations they pursued as adults.

An intriguing finding concerning the parental family life of the elected women legislators is the prevalence of father absence during the formative years of the elected women legislators. Three of the seven elected women legislators, Pak Hyon-suk, Kim Ch'ol-an, and Kim Ok-son, grew up in father-absent homes. The biography of Pak Hyon-suk simply states that her father led a separate life in Sinuiju.[9] Kim Ch'ol-an said she grew up in a fatherless household composed of her mother, two younger sisters, and two paternal aunts-in-law whose husbands were away in Manchuria to fight for national independence. Kim Ok-son also comes from a father-absent family. She remembers seeing her father for the first time during one of his infrequent visits home when she was seven years old. In fact, it was the first and last time she remembers seeing him before his death, which occurred when she was thirteen.

Another three among the elected women legislators, Pak Sun-ch'on, Yim Yong-sin, and Kim Chong-rye, stayed outside paternal influence during their adolescence by living away from home. Thus, only one elected woman legislator, Kim Yun-dok, had grown up under the usual family setting of the parents and children sharing the same roof.

Anthropological research on father absence has focused mainly on its social psychological impact on the boys, suggesting its feminizing effect on the sex identity of the sons.[10] In a similar vein, a more recent study of the effect of mother versus father custody on children's social development suggests that children with the same-sex custodial parent fared better. Thus, girls living under a mother custody arrangement uniformly showed more competent social development than boys in mother custody homes.[11]

The present data on elected women legislators seem to indicate that the absence of fathers had a psychologically positive impact on daughters' initial involvement in the male-dominated world of politics. Generally, it appears that *father absence* for the elected women legislators meant freedom from the patriarchal authority of a father who might very well have prevented his daughter's involvement in the traditionally male occupation of politics by directing her social involvement into a more feminine area. The experiences of the elected women legislators suggest that the liberation from the constraining forces of patriarchal authority vested in the fathers enabled these women to pursue competently and freely the unconventional course of life as political women.

Pak Hyon-suk, for example, never had to worry about how her father would react to her involvement in political activities. Kim Ch'ol-an also did not have to worry about paternal reaction to her participation in public life. She was free to engage in teaching young children and working for the underground independence fighters. In the case of Kim Ok-son, the very absence of a male household head led her to assume the masculine roles in both the domestic and public spheres. For Yim Yong-sin, Pak Sun-ch'on, and Kim Chong-rye, whose fathers shared traditional gender role attitudes and wanted early marriages for their daughters, freedom was won by directly defying paternal authority and by living away from home.

By contrast, eleven of the twenty-two appointed legislators I interviewed stated that they had close relationships with their fathers and that their fathers were positive causal factors for their personal development. They appeared to believe that the presence of a supportive father had bred in them a sense of self-confidence and a strong desire for achievement.

An appointed assemblywoman who had served for two terms stated that her close emotional and intellectual relationship with her father helped her understand and acquire "masculine ways of thinking" and that she felt self-confident and comfortable working with men.

Another appointed assemblywoman who served for two terms also had a very close relationship with her father. She was the first child and had four younger brothers. Her mother had lived separately for health reasons for several years and died when the informant was in college. Her mother often disagreed with her father about how to raise their only daughter.

Her mother wanted to mold her into a virtuous woman in the traditional manner, while her father encouraged her to be rational and independent. The daughter spoke of her father warmly and said that she owed him a great deal for her success.

A third assemblywoman, appointed for two terms, who had a very close relationship with her father said that her father and her older brother did not get along well. The father bestowed his love and attention on his second child, who was his *changnyo* (first daughter).[12] The father advised his daughter to study law and pursue the legal profession or to serve in the government. She said that her father was deeply disappointed with her "small scale" when she decided to major in pharmacology. However, even though she did not study law, she never forgot her father's wish, which she said was at the root of her eventual participation in national politics. Before her legislative appointment, she had been involved in community affairs of the ward where she had lived for more than two decades. She thought her volunteer work for her community was a major factor in her appointment to the National Assembly.

The question that excites our curiosity at this juncture concerns these supportive fathers. One wonders whether it is their affectionate nature, their education, or structural factors of the family that turn men into supportive fathers of their daughters. Also, one might probe the quality of their family life in order to find out what turns a man into a supportive father: Are they dissatisfied husbands or disappointed fathers of unruly sons who try to obtain psychological compensation by bestowing special love and attention on their daughters?

The nature and extent of paternal influences on child socialization and the characteristics of *supportive fathers* need to be further investigated. What I propose here is that *supportive fathers with an egalitarian world view* provide their daughters with "anticipatory socialization," which engenders in them the attitudinal and behavioral preparation for status shifts. It has been suggested that the functions of "anticipatory socialization" are (1) to aid the rise of an individual into a group to which the individual aspires but does not belong, which, in this study, translates into the positive function of a supportive father for a daughter's entry into a high profession; and (2) to ease his or her adjustment after the individual has become part of the profession.[13]

By comparison, it seemed that the mothers of women legislators played a lesser role in their daughters' professional achievements. Among the mothers of elected assemblywomen, only one mother (Kim Ok-son's) seems to have provided strong positive support for the daughter's professional involvement in public life. Others had a more subtle but very strong influence in the feminine role performance of their daughters in the domestic sphere, which is discussed in Chapter 4.

Among the appointed assemblywomen, six mentioned their mother's influence on their occupational achievement. However, two of the six were brought up in a fatherless environment, and for a third informant, the mother served as a negative model, that is, the daughter vowed not to lead a life like her mother's, as a submissive housewife who never voiced her own opinion even when her husband took a concubine. Thus, only three regarded their mothers instead of their fathers as a positive influence for their professional lives, and of the three, only one specifically praised her mother's egalitarian attitude toward and treatment of her siblings, which influenced her own world view. Others mentioned maternal influence, not in terms of modern gender-role attitudes but in terms of unconditional affective support.

The fact that most of the mothers of the main informants belonged to the older generation, which received little formal education, and that none of them were professionals may explain the negligible maternal impact on daughters' professional success.

Birth Order

Adler's belief that firstborn individuals are more achievement-oriented and more often chosen for positions of leadership has led to copious psychological research on the relationship between birth order and intellectual and occupational achievement.[14] Birth order refers to the five basic positions of firstborn, second, middle, youngest, and the only; according to Adler, it tended to have recognizable characteristics later on in life.[15] Researchers have paid special attention to birth order in studying the influence of structural features of the family on women's career development.[16]

In light of the research interest on firstborn children, it is noteworthy that among the seven elected assemblywomen, only one (Kim Ch'ol-an) was the firstborn. There was an only child (Pak Sun-ch'on), and two (Kim Ok-sun and Kim Chong-rye) were the youngest. The remaining three (Yim Yong-sin, Pak Hyon-suk, and Kim Yun-dok) were second daughters, not second children, in large families.[17]

In contrast, the data on appointed legislators reveal the predominance of first daughters. Among the twenty-two appointed ones I interviewed, eight were first daughters. There were four second and four youngest daughters. The remaining six were born into the ordinal positions that may be regarded as the "middle" in the birth order model.[18]

What, then, is the significance, if any, of the predominance of first daughters among the appointed women legislators in contrast to the scarcity of first daughters among the elected ones? Admittedly, the number of cases is too small to make any meaningful generalization.

Nevertheless, the findings may well be explained by sociocultural considerations.

Because birth order is just one of the structural factors in the family, its effect on personal development should be examined in a more holistic manner. Other factors, such as the sex ratio of siblings and birth order within one's own sex, also need to be taken into consideration, since the parental expectations of a child may vary according to different structural compositions of particular families.

Koreans, for example, designate separate birth orders for each sex. Thus, *changnam*, the first son, may have been born after one or more daughters. The same is true of *changnyo*, the first daughter, who may have been born as the first girl after one or more boys were born consecutively.

The first son is expected to inherit the family headship as well as the family property. The family headship involves, among other things, the responsibility to observe ancestor worship. The first son has his social role well delineated by cultural norms. Traditionally, he was not in a position to explore new roles. The younger sons, however, were freer and given far less training in responsibility than their eldest brother.[19] Thus, the fact that there were few eldest sons (*changnam*) of rural *yangban* families among the lists of high achievers in traditional Korea was explained by the cultural role expectations of the eldest sons to stay home and succeed to their family headship.[20] In modern rural Korea, where ambitious farmers sell their cattle and land to send one son to college, they often choose younger sons.[21]   Henderson asserted that one factor in student demonstrations was "the presence of many younger brothers in colleges" who were trained to "demand of others and [were] given far less training in responsibility than the eldest brother."[22]

In comparison, the eldest daughter is said to be a "household asset" (*sallim mitch'on*).[23] She is expected to help the mother with housekeeping chores and with the care of younger siblings. As she grows up, she is thoroughly socialized to the female role by being a constant companion and helper to her mother. Like her eldest brother, she too has little room left for deviating from her traditional role of being an assistant to her mother and often a surrogate mother to her younger siblings. Hence it is not surprising that we do not find many firstborn women in such a non-traditional profession as politics.

In addition to birth order, patterns of parent-child interaction and the cultural context in which structural factors of the family operate (as evidenced in the differential patterns of paternal influence discussed above) should also be counted as important variables for the psychosocial development of an individual. Furthermore, in our interpretation of the findings on Korean female legislators, we should first bear in mind the changes in social environment from the colonial period to the independent nation and the different patterns and processes in the occupational achievements of elected versus appointed women legislators.

A major factor to remember is the fact that prior to their appointments, most of the appointed women legislators were engaged in occupations perceived to be appropriate to their gender, such as administering women's organizations or teaching at colleges. In view of the theories on firstborn girls as "achievers with conservative attitudes,"[24] therefore, it is not surprising that more first daughters were found among the appointed women legislators, who were achievers in traditionally "feminine" occupations,[25] than among the elected women legislators, who were achievers in the traditionally "masculine" sphere.

At the same time, the great proportion of first daughters among appointed women legislators—who belong to the second generation—is a reflection of social change in general and of changing parental expectations of first daughters' roles in particular. Indeed, the fact that six of eight first daughters had close relationships with their fathers, whose supportive guidance and high expectations provided an impetus for their daughters' professional success, suggests that changes have been taking place in the patterns of intrafamily relations.

To sum up, the data on women legislators of this study offer support for the theories on the *firstborn girl* as an achiever with conservative attitudes in that there was a predominance of first daughters among the appointed women legislators, who were selected among women achievers in traditionally "feminine" occupations, while there was a scarcity of first daughters among the elected ones, who achieved their positions in the traditionally "masculine" sphere through election.

The data further indicated that the father-daughter relationship rather than the birth order per se was a major variable in the family structure for the professional achievements of women.

Social Class

Politics, as a prestigious profession, often draws its main actors from leading families of the upper class. More than 50 percent of the male Korean legislators of the seventh National Assembly, for instance, were reported to be of upper-class origins, and another 41 percent were of upper-middle-class backgrounds.[26]

However, the class origin of Korean female legislators presents a different picture. It is noteworthy that none of the elected women legislators came from the upper-class families in Seoul, which for centuries has been the center stage of social and political life of the country.[27] Only one (Pak Hyon-suk) was born and raised in an urban environment in P'yongyang. One half of the remaining six (Yim Yong-sin, Pak Sun-ch'on, and Kim Chong-rye) came from rural areas, while the other half (Kim Ch'ol-an, Kim Ok-son, and Kim Yun-dok) were born in small cities. As to the economic status of the family, one (Kim Chong-rye) experienced poverty in her family life, while another (Yim Yong-sin) came from a wealthy gentry family. The remaining five were from middle-class families.

The predominantly middle-class origins of elected women legislators may be contrasted, for instance, with events in Japan, where "not a few" women Diet members of the early postwar wave came "from upper or noble classes."[28] The absence of upper-class women among the pioneer women legislators in Korea may reflect the social and political history of Korea during the last century. In Korea, it was the "disinherited intellectual class" that eagerly sought modernization,[29] while in Japan, it was the ruling class that led the modernization movement. Moreover, the changes in political recruitment, which took place under the Hungson Taewon'gun in the latter half of the nineteenth century, started the process of undermining the leadership class of the Yi dynasty, and Japanese rule brought its final elimination. Japan controlled all access to power, and Japanese nationals occupied almost all important positions. Politically, Korea had become "a country without a leadership class"[30] by the time the March First Movement took place in 1919. The independence movement, in which only a small proportion (probably 5 percent or less) of the population was involved, provided a new channel to social status and political leadership.[31]

Another explanatory variable, which is applicable to both pioneer- and second-generation women legislators, is the force of gender-role ideology, which exerts differential influences on women and men of different classes in their attitudes toward professional careers. For example, in France, the higher the class, the more prevalent is the perception of incompatibility between family obligations and professional life for married women. Therefore, there is "a greater tendency for women professionals to come from the *classe moyenne,* who are more disposed to utilize higher education as a means of social mobility and comparatively less inhibited by such values."[32] Likewise, in Korea, where the upper class upholds more conservative attitudes concerning gender-role ideology, middle-class families have been more receptive to the democratic principle of sexual equality and have encouraged their women to enter public life.[33]

Among the appointed women legislators, eighteen were from middle-class backgrounds, while four may be regarded to have come from upper-class origins in terms of social prestige or wealth of their families. Not surprisingly, all four women of upper-class origins were engaged in respectable, "feminine" professions prior to their involvement in political life.

Two of the four indicated that they were from upper-class (*yangban*) families in Seoul during our discussions on their education and marriage. One of them, who is a writer and has never married, said that she studied at Suk Myong Girls' School, which was established by Lady Om in 1906. She added that no *yangban* family sent their daughters to Ewha Girls' School, which was founded by a foreign missionary in 1886, because its student body in the early days was composed of concubines and other low-class girls.[34]

The other appointed woman legislator of *yangban* family said that her marriage to a northerner of humble origin was possible only because the country was going through a transitional period in which class distinctions became less important. She met her future husband at a college function, and both of them hold doctorates from universities in the United States. The husband served as a high government official under the Park administration, and the wife was working as a professor before her appointment to the National Assembly.

A third informant said with pride that her father was a provincial representative whose name is listed in the Korean Who's Who. She had taught school and worked as an administrator of a large women's organization before she joined a political party and was appointed to the National Assembly. The fourth informant stated that she came from a wealthy family in Seoul. She was a professor before her appointment to the legislature.

EDUCATION

A significant aspect of formal education for women of this study, especially for the pioneer-generation legislators, as shown in the following pages, is that it provided an environment—away from the confining walls of their homes—in which girls could interact with their peers, form lifelong friendship networks, learn the power of group action in social life, and meet influential teachers.

Some informants, for instance, mentioned during the interviews the importance of meeting a particular mentor at school or a sponsor through extracurricular activities, whose advice had decisive influence in their lives. One appointed assemblywoman said that she has kept contact with her elementary school teacher, whose academic advice enabled her to attend the prestigious Kyonggi Girls' High School, which led to her eventually receiving graduate training in the United States. Another informant mentioned that meeting a Christian sponsor at college was a most significant factor for her professional life. For those informants who received higher education in a coed environment, education provided opportunities to build social networks of "senior/junior" (*sonbae/hubae*) relationships with male students, which would serve as invaluable social resources for their successful professional lives.

Modern education for Korean women was started during the enlightenment period (1876-1910), when a Christian missionary founded the first school for women, Ewha Haktang, in 1886.[35] The three pioneer-generation women legislators were born around the turn of the century and received their education at girls' schools established by Christian missionaries, as described below.

Pak Hyon-suk (1896-1980) attended Sungui Girls' School, run by Christian missionaries in P'yongyang.[36] According to her biography, the confiscation of Korean history books by the Japanese authorities in her school was etched in her memory as a greatly shocking and sorrowful experience for her.[37] Young Hyon-suk made up her mind then to devote herself to "loving the nation and the people" (*aeguk aejok*). She became the leader of the Pine and Bamboo Society (Song Juk Hoe), which was an association of Sungui students who vowed to be as unchanging as the evergreen pine and as upright as the bamboo in their fight for national independence from the Japanese.[38] Their main activity was to secretly collect funds by various means to help the underground resistance groups in their efforts for national independence. After graduating from Sungui in March, 1915, Pak Hyon-suk went to Chonju, a city in the southern part of the country, to teach at Kijon Girls' School (which was also established by Christian missionaries).

Included among her students at Kijon Girls' School was Yim Yong-sin (1899-1977), who had come to Kijon in the fall of the previous year. Yim Yong-sin's father was an enlightened man who helped build a church in the village.[39] With regard to female education, however, he harbored a traditional attitude. He believed that daughters need only learn homemaking skills before their marriage. Little Yong-sin wanted to attend school so badly that she managed for a few days to slip away from home to the school. But when the rumor reached her father, he severely punished her by a ruthless flogging. The only place she was allowed to go was the church.

It was at the church that she learned how to read. She studied by herself, reading the Bible and the books that her brothers studying in Seoul sent her occasionally. Among them, she was most impressed by a book on Joan of Arc. She wanted to become the Joan of Arc of Korea. When she was twelve years old, her father wanted to marry her off, but Yong-sin resisted.

When she was fourteen, Miss Golden, a missionary at Kijon Girls' School in Chonju, visited the church in her village. Yong-sin went to see her and pleaded to her tearfully to help her study at Kijon. Her father, however, was adamantly opposed to the idea of a girl leaving her home to study. Yong-sin finally won her father's permission by staging a four-day hunger strike. When she left the village, accompanied by her father in September of 1914, it was a historical event for the villagers, because no girl before her had ever left the village to go to school. However, none could ever imagine then that Yong-sin would grow up to represent the country at the United Nations and become the first woman to be appointed to the inaugural cabinet of the Republic of Korea.

At Kijon, there were thirty students and five teachers, two of whom were Japanese. Teaching of the Korean language and history was forbidden. During her first winter vacation, Yong-sin came to meet Pastor Kim In-jon, who was the father of her classmate Kim Yon-sil. Her autobiography indicates how deeply impressed Yong-sin was by the egalitarian atmosphere of family life at Pastor Kim's house and by the way he spoke to Yong-sin as an equal human being. Yim wrote: "It was the first time I had been addressed like this by any Korean man. I did not have to keep my eyes on the floor, as was the custom of Korean girls when being spoken to by a man not in their immediate family."[40] When Pastor Kim asked Yong-sin what her ambition was, after a moment's silence, she blurted out: "I want to save Korea."[41] During that winter vacation, she learned through Pastor Kim the details of Korean history and was also informed of the resistance movement.

When school began, Yim Yong-sin and her friends requested that their teachers give them courses in Korean history. When refused, she and her three closest friends decided to make a copy of a Korean history book. She then went to Pastor Kim to borrow a history book from him. After warning her that if the Japanese found her with the book, they would "chop off" her head, and that he would also be placed in a dangerous position, Pastor Kim lent a copy of *Tongguk Yoksa* (Oriental History) to Yong-sin. Yong-sin and her friends labored for months over their secret task of making copies. As soon as a copy was finished, they smuggled it out of the school grounds and Pastor Kim helped them get it into the hands of secret study circles that later became centers of the resistance movement. Before long, their clandestine activities came under suspicion by the school authorities, and they had to bury the book. Yim wrote in her autobiography that "it was my first weapon in my fight against the hated masters of my country."[42]

When Pak Hyon-suk came to Kijon as a teacher in the spring of 1915, she joined a student prayer group composed of patriotic students, including Yim Yong-sin. Pak led the group until she returned to her alma mater to teach in 1917. The group, which came to be known as the "suicide squad," successfully managed a boycott against singing the Japanese national anthem and bowing in front of the Emperor's picture.

They infuriated the Japanese teachers by puncturing the eyes in the pictures of the Japanese emperor hung in every classroom.

To the "Suicide Squad" the Japanese were not the only enemy; ancient Korean customs such as the wearing of the women's *ssugaech'ima* "veil" had to be fought. *Ssugaech'ima* (over-the-head skirt) is a full-length shawl which women had to wear over their heads to conceal their faces when going outside their homes. The shape was the same as the skirt. The belt of the skirt was worn over the head and around the face, and grasped under the chin.[43] Students in girls' schools began to discard the *ssugaech'ima* around the turn of the century.[44]

Yim wrote that *ssugaech'ima* was not only inconvenient but also emphasized the fact "that females could not take an equal place in the community. Imagine a *sigachima*-clad[45] girl commanding the respect of male associates!"[46] They audaciously requested the school authorities to abolish the custom of wearing *ssugaech'ima*, which shocked the teachers and resulted in the dismissal of five students from the school. To save them, the group urged the whole student body to go on strike. Eventually, parents had to be called in for the matter to be resolved in their favor.

After her graduation in 1918, Yim went to the mining village of Yangdae-ri to teach at the Yangdae Elementary School. In addition to her duties as a teacher, she engaged in enlightening and improving the lives of the village residents.

Yim Yong-sin further studied both in Japan and in the United States (at the University of Southern California). She left for Japan for further education in November, 1919, two months after she was sentenced to a stay of execution for three and a half years for her participation in the March First Movement. She returned to Korea in 1921 with a diploma from Hiroshima Christian College. She began teaching at Kongju High School and resumed resistance activities. Her speech at the Kongju Young Men's Association in October, 1921, angered the Japanese police, who suspended her teaching license. Yim Yong-sin then decided to go to the United States upon the completion of her probation and started to prepare herself by learning English at Ewha Christian College in Seoul. She received an M.A. in theology from the University of Southern California in 1931.[47]

Pak Sun-ch'on—who served in the National Assembly for five terms—was born in a village in Tongnae county in South Kyongsang province in 1898.[48] Her given name, in fact, was Myong-ryon. But, she came to be known as *Sunch'on-daek* (a married woman from Sunch'on) since the days of her fugitive life after the March First Movement of 1919. She finally adopted the alias as her legal given name in 1960.

Pak Sun-ch'on was fortunate to have a father who thought daughters needed to be educated. She attended a private academy, dressed like a boy, to learn Chinese classics. Pak wrote in her autobiographical essays that she grew up as a tomboy, playing with her classmates, who were all boys.[49] She was baptized at the age of ten. Then, at the recommendation of a Western Catholic priest who visited her village from time to time, her father decided to send his young daughter to Ilsin Girls' School in the provincial capital of Pusan (the second largest city in Korea). It was about twenty kilometers from her village,[50] and her father hired a villager to carry little Sun-ch'on on his back to the school. Since it was the first time she had been separated from her parents, Sun-ch'on became homesick and found her dormitory life too lonesome. She quietly slipped out of the school and returned home. In a little while, however, she started missing her school. So she decided to go back to school and walked by herself all the way to the school without telling her parents. As she grew more accustomed to her school life, she began to lead her classmates in playing practical jokes on her Japanese teachers, and scratched the portrait of the Japanese Emperor and Empress hung in the teachers' room to make them look as if they were crying. When she was seventeen, her father wanted to marry her off. Sun-ch'on, with her secret dream to become the Joan of Arc of Korea, however, refused to get married, and her irate father stopped sending her money. With the help of a sympathetic missionary teacher, she was able to win the fight by holding out for five months without financial assistance from her father.[51] After her graduation, Pak Sun-ch'on also started working as a teacher at Masan Girls' School in 1917.

Pak Sun-ch'on further studied at a women's college in Tokyo, Japan. The reason she chose to go to Tokyo disguised as a Japanese woman was to evade the imprisonment for her participation in the March First Movement. A few months after she matriculated at a woman's medical school in Tokyo in 1920, her true identity was revealed to the Japanese police. After spending a year in prison in Masan, Korea, she went back to Tokyo and studied social work.

What is significant about these episodes is that each of these women began to take leadership roles in a school environment. Also, for Pak Sun-ch'on and Yim Yong-sin, dormitory life at school meant the opportunity to grow up free of patriarchal authority, which is a powerful source of social and psychological restraint on women's lives. Both of them in fact defied their fathers' wishes that they marry, and both won their psychological battles. These experiences of self-assertion, I think, must have helped them in strengthening their characters and in acquiring perceptions of the world based on "internal control."[52]

The other pioneer-generation elected woman legislator, Kim Ch'ol-an (1912-92) was basically self-educated and took a correspondence course from Meiji University in Japan. She then passed the national qualifying examination to become a preschool teacher. Years later, after she retired from the political arena, Kim Ch'ol-an studied international politics at the graduate school of Song Kyun Kwan University in Seoul. The level of education of the pioneer-generation women legislators, seen in a socio-historical context in which 90 percent of the female population were illiterate,[53] puts them into an educational elite.

Of the three elected women legislators of the second generation, two received higher education, while the remaining one received minimal formal education. Kim Ok-son majored in political science at Chungang University (which was founded by Yim Yong-sin). She further studied the subject by doing Ph.D. coursework at her alma mater. Kim Yun-dok majored in law at Song Kyun Kwan University. For Kim Chong-rye, the special training class at Tamyang Girls' High School, held for a year right after liberation, was the extent of her formal education.

On the one hand, the case of Kim Chong-rye illustrates that politics is one profession that does not require a specific background or level of formal education. On the other hand, it also reflects the generally deprived social conditions under which the majority of the women of her generation lived, straddling the transitional period of the latter part of the colonial rule and the postliberation disorder. It should be noted here that although she lacks formal education, Kim Chong-rye is gifted with high intelligence and oratorical talents, and her military training and political socialization under the tutelage of Yi Pom-sok, the first prime minister of the Republic of Korea, provided her with a sense of self-confidence and practical advantage for her political career.

The generational differences in educational backgrounds of the elected women legislators were most remarkable in the subjects they studied and their experiences in receiving education abroad. None of the pioneer-generation women legislators studied law or political science, the major subjects of two of the second-generation elected women legislators (Kim Ok-son and Kim Yun-dok). None of the second-generation elected women legislators received education abroad, while two of the pioneer-generation women legislators (Yim Yong-sin and Pak Sun-ch'on) received higher education overseas.

That education is a crucial factor for social mobility was most saliently manifested in the educational backgrounds of the appointed legislators. Not only did all appointed women legislators receive higher education, but nearly half of them (ten of the twenty-two) had studied in the United States. Another significant fact is that half of the twelve informants who did not experience overseas schooling pursued postgraduate training in Korea. Altogether, fifteen of the twenty-two informants (68 percent) received graduate training. Their educational achievement stands out in stark contrast to the national average of the number of school years for women, which was 6.63 years as of 1980.[54]

There were five Ph.D. degree holders (three in political science, one in history, and one in public health) and a medical doctor. Except for the medical doctor, all of the five women received their doctoral degrees in the United States. With regard to undergraduate majors, four studied law, four political science, and three English literature. For the remaining eleven, the subjects ranged from home economics, French literature, music, fine arts, and physical education to economics, medicine, and pharmacology.

The comparison of the educational characteristics of the female appointed legislators with those of the fifty-five appointed male legislators of the Democratic Justice Party in the twelfth National Assembly revealed some noticeable sex differences in the subject of their study.[55]

The most salient sex difference was seen in the two subjects of military science and public administration, which none of the women legislators of this study had taken up. Public administration apparently is perceived as another male domain. Seven of the nine male legislators who studied the subject took it up in addition to law, business, economics, or military science. To recall a statistical report mentioned in Chapter 1, the percentage of women in administrative and managerial positions drastically declined from 18.9 percent in 1960 to 1.5 percent in 1980. In any case, it was not until 1973 that a woman passed the national examination for higher civil service.[56]

All the appointed male legislators received higher education and training. Nine of them (16 percent) went to military academies, and four of these nine furthered their education by receiving postgraduate training. Altogether, twenty-two of the fifty-five (40 percent) received some form of graduate education. There were ten Ph.D. holders, among whom four had studied political science. Law was the most popular subject of study among the appointed male legislators of the twelfth National Assembly; nineteen (35 percent) majored in law. Political science was second in popularity, with nine legislators who majored in it (16 percent). Others' major subjects ranged from business, economics, philosophy, music, and education to engineering, pharmacology, medicine, and veterinary science.

Twenty-three men (42 percent) had overseas educational experiences; eleven in the United States, seven in Japan, four in Europe, one in China, and one in India.[57] In terms of the ratio, their female colleagues had a higher percentage of U.S. educational experiences. Three of the five appointed female legislators of the twelfth National Assembly had graduate training in the United States. It is interesting to note that two of the three enjoyed assignments to the prestigious Foreign Policy Committee of the National Assembly.[58] One had been a professor of history and the other an administrator of a large women's organization before their appointments to the legislature. According to one of them, the Foreign

Policy Committee is regarded as "the Senate" of the National Assembly. Their ability to speak the English language undoubtedly was an important factor for the assignments, because they often have to deal with foreign counterparts and to represent the Korean legislature at international conferences.

NOTES

1. See, for example, Clark and Clark (1986); Kelly and Boutilier (1978); Kirkpatrick (1974); Means (1972); and Pharr (1981).

2. Kirkpatrick (1974).

3. Means (1972).

4. Pharr (1981:115).

5. Clark and Clark (1986).

6. Hennig and Jardim (1977); Lebra (1981).

7. Crandall and Crandall (1983).

8. Thornton, Duane, and Camburn (1983).

9. Sungui Publication Committee (SPC) (1968:166).

10. Burton and Whiting (1961); D'Andrade (1973). See also Parker, Smith, and Ginat (1975) for a dissenting argument.

11. Santrock and Warshak (1979).

12. See the section on birth order below.

13. Merton (1957:265).

14. Adler (1924). For surveys of birth order literature, see Miley (1969); Vockell, Felker, and Miley (1973); and Forer (1977).

15. Adler (1964); Shulman and Mosak (1977).

16. Hennig and Jardim (1977); Kammeyer (1966); H. S. Yi (1984); and Rossi (1965).

17. See the following page for a discussion of the Korean system of birth order designation.

18. For a discussion of the problems of the birth order description of the "middle" child in large families (e.g., in a family of four siblings), see Shulman and Mosak (1977:117-18).

19. The situation was apparently the same in Japan. See Nakayama (1985:viii) for a biographical sketch of Fukuzawa Yukichi (1835-1901), a second son who founded Keio University.

20. T. Kim (1964).

21. Henderson (1968:221).

22. Henderson (1968:439).

23. The proverbial phrase often serves to comfort disappointed parents whose first child is a girl. For more Korean proverbs about women, see Tieszen (1977).

24. Kammeyer (1966); Rossi (1965).

25. A study of Korean women professors (H. S. Yi 1984) also noted the predominance of firstborn daughters among its sample.

26. Kim and Pai (1981).

27. For a description of Seoul as the symbol of centralization in the Yi dynasty, see Henderson (1968:29-33).

28. Jones (1975:721).

29. Chung (1961:26).

30. Henderson (1968:77).

31. For more discussion on the class origin of Korean political men from the late nineteenth century to the beginning of the Republic of Korea, see Henderson (1968:59-147).

32. Silver (1973:85).

33. For a further discussion on the middle-class background of women politicians, see the section on the meaning of legislative career in Chapter 8.

34. See Y. Kim (1979:227).

35. Y. Kim (1979:217-21).

36. The life history of Pak Hyon-suk as presented in this book is based on her biography (SPC 1968), newspaper articles, and my interviews with her granddaughter, a longtime friend and a writer of biographies of many famous Koreans.

37. The colonial government confiscated all textbooks written by Koreans in November, 1910 (Dong-a Ilbosa 1985:24).

38. Pine and bamboo, representing personal integrity and loyalty, are the two most popular cultural symbols and are much utilized in poems and paintings.

39. The source materials concerning the life history of Yim Yong-sin as presented in this book include her autobiography (Yim 1951), the biographies (PCC 1959; Son 1972), Korea Women's Association (KWA) (1986), and newspaper articles.

40. Yim (1951:57).

41. Yim (1951:57).

42. Yim (1951:62).

43. According to Y. Kim (1979:148), *ssugaech'ima* was made of light blue cotton. According to Ha (1958:71), however, it was dark green, pale blue, or white.

44. Y. Kim (1979:276).

45. *Sigachima*, I think, is Cholla dialect for *ssugaech'ima*.

46. Yim (1951:68).

47. Son (1972:256).

48. The source materials on the life history of Pak Sun-ch'on as described in this book include autobiographical essays (Pak 1968; Pak 1974-75), a biography (Ch'oe 1972), magazine articles (T. Yi 1986; C. Yim 1985), and newspaper interview articles.

49. Pak (1974-75).

50. Pak (1974-75) wrote that it was fifty *li*. Since ten *li* by the traditional unit of measurement is equivalent to the modern unit of one *i* (or *li*) (which is 3.9273 kilometers), fifty *li* is translated as twenty kilometers.

51. Pak (1974-75:3).

52. Crandall and Crandall (1983).

53. H. Yi (1982:442).

54. KWDI (1985:75).

55. The information on the male legislators was drawn from National Assembly (NA) (1985).

56. Chon Chae-hi, the first woman to pass the national examination for higher civil service in 1973, was a section chief in the Ministry of Labor in 1985.

57. One had studied both in Japan and West Germany, which explains why the sum of the numbers of each category is twenty-four.

58. The two are Kim Hyon-ja (in the eleventh National Assembly) and Kim Yong-jong (in the twelfth National Assembly).

4

Other Personal Characteristics

Are women politicians "ordinary women" in their private lives, fulfilling the traditional female roles of mothers and housewives? A study of women legislators of the United States suggested that they are "feminine" women in the traditional sex-stereotyped sense of the term and that they accept and embody the traditional role definitions in all aspects but one—that of being a legislator.[1] 90 percent of the U.S. congresswomen between 1917 and 1964, for example, were married.[2] In comparison, the ratio of married women among my sample was rather low (72 percent), in spite of the more negative cultural evaluation of unmarried people in Korea than in the United States.[3]

Social respectability for a professional woman in Korea still derives mainly from her marital status and her reputation as a virtuous woman who has fulfilled her traditional roles as a daughter, daughter-in-law, wife, and mother. An appointed woman legislator flatly stated that "in our culture, single people are regarded as 'half persons.'" The negative image of being single, for example, led a prominent journalist turned social activist to deny being single when asked by a college student for an interview during a study on single women. She is reported to have said, "I am not single; I live with my parents."[4]

MARRIAGE

When cultural ideology puts a premium on being married, as in Korean society, the problem of balancing marriage and career weighs heavily on professional women. One core informant remembered her rebellious reaction to Helen Kim's speech during the commencement ceremony at Ewha Women's University. She said Kim, the first Korean woman to receive a Ph.D., who devoted her life to women's education and never married, warned the graduating class of 1961 about the incompatibility between career and family for women and advised them to choose between the two. Almost a quarter of a century later, career women's problems remain unresolved. Having experienced a late marriage that ended in divorce, my informant confessed that she now appreciated Kim's wisdom about the matter.

Five of the seven elected women legislators were married when they ran for a legislative seat. One was never married, and another was divorced. The mode of marriage was predominantly an arranged one. The number of children varied from none or one to many. As to the marital status of appointed legislators, 73 percent (sixteen of the twenty-two informants) were married at the time of their appointments. The remaining 27 percent comprised five single women and one divorced woman. The divorcee subsequently remarried a widowed pastor—they knew each other from childhood—during the period of her legislative tenure. One of the five single women, who was a professor, also was married during her tenure but divorced soon thereafter. The other four unmarried appointed legislators included a professor, a government official, a journalist-turned-writer, and a reporter-turned-partisan respectively before their legislative appointments. The subject of marriage was a very sensitive one for them, and none of them really wanted to discuss their private life as single women.

Supportive Husbands

A remarkable fact about the marriages of appointed assemblywomen is that 81 percent (thirteen of the sixteen) of the appointed women legislators who were married at the time of their appointment indicated that their marriage was a "love marriage" rather than the traditional arranged one, and that their husbands were very understanding and supportive of their professional career.

One informant told me that it was in fact at the urging of her husband that she took up medicine. She acknowledged with gratitude that the moral and financial support of her husband was an indispensable factor for the success of her professional life. She recalled that, on the commencement day when she received an M.D. degree, her professor, who congratulated her with a bouquet, asked her to let him finally have the honor of meeting her "uncommonly supportive and understanding husband."

Indeed, having a supportive husband seemed a prerequisite for the successful career development of married women in this study. In fact, a cooperative husband seems the first requirement for married women politicians across cultures to successfully juggle family and career.[5] Realizing the critical importance of a supportive husband for a married career woman, Kim Yun-dok said that her advice to young women with political ambition had been, "Come see me with your husband after your marriage." She herself has a very supportive husband, who actively participated in the election campaign for his wife.

The husband of Pak Hyon-suk, Kim Song-op, was the first director of the P'yongyang branch of the *Dong-a Ilbo* (a major vernacular daily), and their marriage, which took place in September, 1919, was regarded as a union of two patriots.[6] At their wedding in a church in P'yongyang, they were dressed in traditional Korean dress (*hanbok*), made of indigenously produced cotton,[7] which symbolized their patriotic commitment to work for the independence of their country. In 1938, Kim became paralyzed and impotent as the result of torture by the Japanese colonial police for his involvement in the underground resistance movement. Pak Hyon-suk inwardly vowed to work a double load on behalf of her invalid husband, whom she looked after for twenty-seven years until his death in 1965.[8]

In the case of Pak Sun-ch'on, her scholar-husband Pyon Hi-yong seemed to have played an important role in the illustrious political career of his wife with his steadfast support and wise counsel. According to a male informant who had a close relationship with the couple, Pyon played the role of a private sounding board to his wife for her political actions. When Pak Sun-ch'on came under criticism for her personal friendship with the First Lady Yuk Yong-su (Mrs. Park Chung Hee) after her retirement from political life (see Chapter 8), she reportedly stated that had her husband been alive, his wise advice could have kept her from taking such actions, which were being misunderstood and criticized.[9]

Pak Sun-ch'on wrote that her secret dream of becoming the Joan of Arc of Korea made her remain single until her late twenties.[10] Pak Sun-ch'on was fortunate to marry Pyon Hi-yong, a fellow Korean student in Japan, who courted her "with fervent passion" and steadfastly supported her political career during their marital life. Pyon, in fact, had been on the list of Sun-ch'on's father as one of three eligible bachelors for a son-in-law and was a participant in the Korean Youth Independence Corps that met at the YMCA Hall in Kanda, Tokyo, on February 8, 1919, and issued a declaration demanding independence for their country.[11]

When Sun-ch'on wanted to return to Tokyo in 1920 after serving a year in prison for her participation in the March First Movement, her father approved her plan on condition that she marry Pyon. Sun-ch'on was so eager to return to Tokyo that she consented to her father's condition even though she had intended to remain single and devote her life to serving the country.

When their wedding took place in Seoul in December, 1925, Pak was twenty-seven and Pyon thirty-one. Their marriage was regarded as a late one in those days. After their wedding in Seoul, the couple went back to Tokyo so that Pak Sun-ch'on could finish her studies. She gave birth to her first son during the last semester before her graduation. Pyon was a Catholic, and he and Pak Sun-ch'on had seven children altogether. The marital life of Pak Sun-ch'on appeared the most ideal for women who want to balance their marital life and political career. It seemed that Pak Sun-ch'on never let her traditional female role performance prevent her from participating in political life, and her supportive and respectable scholar-husband was always there as her private sounding board.

In contrast, the two suitors of Yim Yong-sin turned out to be married men, to whom her family objected. Yim Yong-sin was finally married at the age of thirty-nine to Han Su-kyo,[12] a businessman residing in Los Angeles, whom she met during her trip to the United States to raise funds for Chungang University. Han, who apparently did not share her conviction that Korea would regain its independence soon, objected to his wife's sending all the educational funds she raised to Korea. The lack of support from her husband for her work disappointed Yim Yong-sin greatly.

When she heard the news of the German invasion of Poland in September, 1939, she thought the war might soon spread to other parts of the world and affect Korea. She wanted to return to Korea immediately, but her husband did not. Yim Yong-sin finally left the United States in May, 1940, after she received a telegram from her family in Seoul to come back soon. Her husband promised to join her in Seoul as soon as he took care of his business in Los Angeles. Neither of them knew then that that would be the end of their marriage. They had no children of their own.[13]

Yim Yong-sin, who dedicated her energy to politics, education, and women's rights, sometimes felt slighted by her male colleagues due to her marital status and resented it, according to my informant. Yim Yong-sin remained single and adopted Yim Ch'ol-sun (a son of her brother), who succeeded her as president of Chungang University upon her retirement in 1972.[14]

Kim Ch'ol-an, who married a son of a wealthy family, had not only a supportive husband but also the eager endorsement of her father-in-law (see Chapters 5 through 8 for more details). Thus, with the exception of Kim Chong-rye, all elected women legislators who were married at the time of their election had supportive husbands, as their brief profiles portrayed in this chapter showed.

As to Kim Chong-rye, a passionate political activist and active advocate of women's rights, she was married at the age of thirty-two to Yun Chae-su. The bridegroom was the same age and came from the same town as the bride. They had known each other for more than a decade before their wedding. In the meantime, Yun had gone to Japan after the Korean War and established himself as a businessman.

Kim Chong-rye told me that since she wanted to remain single to devote her life to working for the needy, she had ignored his romantic interest in her for a long time. Concerned *sonbae* (seniors) including Kim Ch'ol-an, however, kept advising her to get married. They asserted that marriage would help her to work more effectively.

The choice of marital residence became a problem for them, however. Yun wanted his wife to come and live in Japan, while Kim Chong-rye tried to make him return to Korea. They have been a "separated couple" for more than twenty years. She told me that her unusual marital life became a source of libelous comments and vicious backbiting by her political rivals. Some misinformed adversaries thought that she was the "local wife"[15] of Yun and even tried to exert clandestine pressure on her to either get a divorce or resign from her political office after she became minister of health and social welfare in 1982.

According to my informant, Yun has dutifully paid the household bills for his wife and son in Korea and tries to visit them annually. In the meantime, he has raised a second family in Japan and has refused to consent to his wife's demand for a divorce, citing as his main reason the dishonor it would inflict on their only son. Kim Chong-rye told me that despite her lifelong struggle for women's rights, she felt she was no longer qualified to speak for them because of her peculiar marital circumstances.

The marital situation of Kim Chong-rye symbolically underscores the importance of formality in Korean social life. Even though her conjugal life in reality barely exists, she is legally a married woman with a husband and a son. Her unusual marital circumstance therefore accords her the social respectability of a married woman, but at the same time frees her of wifely duties in the domestic sphere.

Gender-Role Attitudes

A study of causes and consequences of gender-role attitude and attitude change indicated the parental family as having a definite impact on gender-role attitudes of children and asserted that "most of the influence was transmitted through the mother's own attitudes."[16] An examination of feminine role performance and gender-role attitudes among the women legislators of this study seems to provide evidence for the importance of maternal influence in the gender-role attitudes and performances of career women.

For example, Pak Hyon-suk and Kim Ch'ol-an, who were raised in father-absent families and lived with their mothers until their marriage (although Pak spent a couple of years in Chonju as a teacher), appeared to have been very mindful of their mothers' teachings and advice concerning woman's roles. Kim Ch'ol-an told me that whenever things got too tough for her in her marital life, she recalled her mother's advice: "Once a woman is married, she should be prepared to die in her husband's home." Both Pak Hyon-suk and Kim Ch'ol-an were married by arrangement at the age of twenty-two and twenty-three, respectively, and both seemed to have taken great pride in their exemplary fulfillment of the traditional feminine roles. In the case of Kim Ch'ol-an, who was born as the first of three daughters, she indeed showed the characteristics of a first child, including a very traditional orientation toward the feminine role.[17] On the phone as well as during the interview, she underlined the socio-cultural desirability of marriage for career women in terms of its practical advantage. She asserted that "it is only when a woman is married, has experienced childbirth, and is backed by a respectable husband that she appears fully qualified to lead public life."

Kim Yun-dok, who had lived with her parents until her marriage at twenty, emphasized the importance of fulfilling maternal and wifely roles in women's social development and took great pride in having fulfilled scrupulously the traditional female roles of being a good daughter-in-law, wife, and mother. She said cutting down her sleeping hours was her solution to dealing with the double work load of a married career woman.

In the case of Kim Ok-son, who always wears men's attire and has never married, the traditional gender-role attitude of her mother and special family circumstances have resulted in a peculiarly culture-bound manifestation of the traditional gender-role ideology. Kim Ok-son is proud of having fulfilled her mother's expectation of her to be the "son" of the family in place of her only brother, who died during the war.

According to one of my main informants, when the mother of Kim Ok-son saw her daughter in men's attire for the first time, she almost swooned in surprise, mistaking Ok-son for her lost only son. The relationship between mother and daughter seemed to have been one of deep mutual devotion. "One may say that it was a kind of remarriage for the mother," was the surprising comment made by my informant, who came to know Kim Ok-son as a colleague in the ninth National Assembly.

For Kim Ok-son, her assumption of the traditionally male role of the household head made it impossible for her to marry a man. While her mother was living, she seemed to have supplied Kim Ok-son with the kind of moral support that one might expect from a spouse. After I got to know Kim Ok-son better, she expressed her loneliness and wishes for a supportive "wife." One day she told me how envious she felt when she visited a male legislator. She said that her colleague treated her to a very tasty medicinal herbal tea that his wife made him every day. Kim Ok-son told me that she felt she had found the secret of the unusually youthful appearance of her colleague and wished for a caring wife like his.

Through my interviews and various meetings with Representative Kim Ok-son, I learned that the mother treated her youngest daughter with the kind of reverence and care that is customarily reserved for the patriarch of a family. After Kim Ok-son became a college student and began to participate in public life, for example, the mother would no longer address her youngest child by her first name. Instead, the mother expressed her respect for her daughter-son by always attaching an honorific suffix, *nim*, to her social title, such as *sonbi* (scholar)-*nim*, *wonjang* (director)-*nim* or *uiwon* (representative)-*nim*. (In fact, people's names are very personal possessions in Korea. The Koreans in general avoid using the first name of an adult as a term of address in their social interaction. A man is usually addressed by his social or occupational title in non-kin situations, and fictive kinship terms such as uncle, aunt, grandfather, and grandmother are customarily used among strangers. Among acquaintances and relatives, a young unmarried person is referred to as the [first, second, etc.] son or daughter of the such-and-such [surname] family, and after marriage, he or she is addressed as so-and-so's mother or father.)

The mother of Kim Ok-son would order Ok-son's two older sisters not to make any noise when Ok-son was home, especially after a hard day's work. The mother also made sure to procure for Kim Ok-son all kinds of foods, concoctions, and medicinal herbs believed to generate stamina, which are usually consumed by men. The mother died in 1975, and until then Kim Ok-son was quite overweight.

Kim Ok-son on her part was always mindful of her filial duties. She told me that she delighted her mother with the surprise gift of a gold ring and a lavish party in celebration of her *hwan'gap* (sixtieth birthday) by careful long-term planning and saving for the occasion. She was still a teenager then. Her older sisters, in comparison, were unable to contribute much to the festivity. When she finally won a legislative seat, Kim Ok-son attributed her success to the total support and devotion of her mother.[18] When her legislative activities required her to live in Seoul, Kim Ok-son said she never failed to make a long-distance call to her mother (who preferred to stay in their hometown) at least once a day.

In contrast, the other three elected women legislators (Pak Sun-ch'on, Yim Yong-sin, and Kim Chong-rye) who lived away from the influence of the traditional gender role socialization of their mothers appeared to have been much less preoccupied with excelling in their fulfillment of the traditional feminine roles. Kim Chong-rye, who led an independent life away from her parents since her adolescence, and Yim Yong-sin, who had studied in the United States, seemed especially liberated in gender-role attitudes. They all fought against their fathers' authority to contract early marriages, led rather independent lives beginning in adolescence, and made independent decisions concerning their marriages. (However, the marital situations of the three women, as described above, were very different.)

The strong advocacy of traditional role fulfillment as a prerequisite for a woman's entry into politics, as expressed by Kim Ch'ol-an, for example, is not confined to members of the older generation nor to Korean society. For instance, it was reported that a most persistent problem for Takako Doi, the female leader of the Japan Socialist Party, was her unmarried state. During the election campaign for the upper house of Japan's parliament in the summer of 1989, a cabinet minister pointed out that Doi did not have a husband or children and questioned whether such a person could serve as prime minister.[19]   Among the women of this study, an appointed member of the twelfth National Assembly who was in her early forties also stressed the point, pronouncing the image of professional women as "austere old maids" to be a thing of the past. (Among the pioneer-generation professional women, several well-known public figures—such as Helen Kim, Yi Suk-chong, and Ko Hwang-kyong—may be regarded as "austere old maids.") My informant maintained that today women with political ambitions had better attend to their traditional feminine roles first in order to be recognized as eligible for legislative appointment. She said that even though it was at the urging of her husband that she entered political life by running for the National Council for Unification, she was extremely mindful of the possible negative effect of her political career on her family life. She emphasized the importance of fulfilling domestic duties for political women, because she knew that if she were divorced as a result of neglecting her family life, the party would not want her any more.

When confronted with the question of role priority, the married informants, especially appointed lawmakers, almost invariably relegated their extradomestic roles to secondary positions after their domestic ones. Their gender-role attitudes were very traditional. On one hand, it is surprising that their active participation in public life did not translate into changes in their gender-role attitudes in private life. On the other hand, considering that the moral tone of their formal education has been in terms of cultivating womanly virtues,[20] it is no surprise to find that most career women in male-dominant professions adhere to traditional gender-role attitudes in their marital lives. Moreover, the social stigma attached to divorce, especially for women, reinforces the conservative approach to "proper" gender role performance of professional women in their private lives.

Besides, since most of the women have domestic help of various types, they can still advocate and adhere to the traditional sexual division of labor at home and keep the strain of their dual work load at a manageable level. An appointed woman legislator told me that her husband used to share housekeeping and child-care responsibilities when they lived as a student couple in the United States. However, after they returned to Korea, housekeeping and other domestic affairs became the responsibilities of the wife. She said she did weekly grocery shopping while a housemaid prepared meals and took care of other housekeeping chores.

Since the kitchen was a woman's place and off limits to men in traditional Korea, many men in modern Korea, especially men of the older generation, still would not dream of sharing domestic chores with their wives. In addition, the pattern of office work hours causes men to return home late at night, often after eating out with business associates. Thus, the structure of the work world as well as traditional gender-role ideology conspire to leave housework the sole responsibility of the wife even when she also works outside home.

RELIGION

Religion, especially Christianity, constitutes an important element in the personal makeup of my informants. Indeed, the significance of Christianity in the lives of Korean political women is unique. Six of the seven elected women legislators identified themselves as Christians and the remaining one as Buddhist.

Three pioneer political women (Pak Hyon-suk, Pak Sun-ch'on, and Yim Yong-sin) came from Christian families and were christened during their childhood. The husbands of both Pak Hyon-suk and Pak Sun-ch'on were also devout Christians. "The Way to Convert Korean Buddhists to Christianity" was the title of the thesis written by Yim Yong-sin at the University of Southern California in 1931.[21] Pak Hyon-suk was a Presbyterian elder.

Among the three elected women legislators of the postrevolution era, Kim Ok-son exhibits perhaps the most ardent religious commitment as a Christian. She has built and dedicated five churches, is an elder in a Holiness Church in Seoul, and occasionally delivers evangelical speeches to the congregation. She started attending Sunday school at the village church from her childhood and gained not only biblical knowledge but also valuable leadership training there. She then went to Chongsin Girls' School, which was founded by Christian missionaries in Seoul, where she became ill. She was told by a doctor to quit school until she was cured of her tubercular condition. She refused to accept her illness as a fact. Instead she went up to the top of Namsan Hill in Seoul, offered a fervent supplicatory prayer to God, and threw away the medicine the doctor gave her. Miraculously, she said, her health improved, and she was cured of her illness by her faith in God.[22] Kim Ok-son further stated that she learned from reading the Bible how futile life could be if one lived selfishly, only for oneself and one's family. For her, a meaningful life is to work for others.

Kim Yun-dok started to go to church during her high school days. She said she liked occasionally to visit churches other than her own to listen to good sermons by different ministers and draw inspiration from them.

Kim Chong-rye, in contrast, had long resisted her friends' invitation to join them in Christian fellowship. She said she challenged them with the question, "Why is there so much misery in the world if there exists a loving God, as Christianity preaches?" She told me that it was during her years as a political prisoner (see the following section on personality) that she began to seek religious truth. After her release, she gradually turned to Christianity. She stated that nowadays she constantly prays for God's help and guidance to become a more effective leader.

Thus, among the elected women lawmakers, only Kim Ch'ol-an had the more traditional Buddhist religious orientation. She told me that after her first son died young, she visited numerous Buddhist temples to pray for the long life of her second son, who became her only son. The son, now a college law professor, stated that his mother had instilled in her children the motto "to live for others," in accordance with Buddhistic attitudes.

As for the appointed members, 50 percent (eleven of the twenty-two) said they were Christians, while only 9 percent (two of the twenty-two) identified themselves as Buddhists. The remaining 41 percent (nine of the twenty-two appointed women legislators) were nonbelievers. Thus, among the women legislators of this study, 69 percent (twenty out of the twenty-nine) had a religion, and among the twenty religious women lawmakers, 85 percent (seventeen) were Christians.[23]

A survey on Korean national characteristics, conducted jointly by a newspaper company and a Gallup research institute in Seoul, reported that 51.9 percent of the population believed in some religion. Among them, Christians accounted for 24.4 percent (Protestants for 17.9 percent and Catholics for 6.5 percent), Buddhists for 26.2 percent, and others for 1.3 percent.[24] In view of the fact that Buddhists outnumber Christians in Korea, the unusually high proportion of Christians (58.6 percent) among the sample of this study is most remarkable.

It is a generally accepted view that Christian churches assumed the leadership of the modernization movement in Korea. The influence of Christian churches on Korean society was especially pronounced during the period of Japanese occupation.[25] Koreans reacted to the forced assimilation policy (such as imposition of Shintoism as the national religion) by turning more to Christianity. Christian churches not only helped fill the religious needs of the people but also became the center of political action. Since religious institutions were relatively free from harsh suppression by the Japanese colonial government until the mid-1930s,

Christian churches were convenient meeting places for the participants in the Independence Movement. Christian churches hence served as a new ladder of social mobility, especially for men who did not belong to *yangban* (upper-class) families, and produced "political Christians" such as Syngman Rhee, Kim Kyu-sik, Yo Un-hyong, and Cho Pyong-ok.[26]

The *yangban* generally eschewed the church. A major reason perhaps lay in the fundamental clash of Confucian values of avoidance of labor and the cultivation of physical immobility against the Protestant ethic of the sacredness of work.[27] Men in general, and *yangban* in particular, were able to put the Confucian values into practice and avoid physical labor. However, women as housekeepers could not afford the luxury of physical immobility. This gender-role difference may partially account for the political women of the pioneer generation embracing Christian ways of life more wholeheartedly than their male counterparts. For instance, it was Pak Sun-ch'on who worked hard on her family farm while her scholar husband pored over his books. In addition, she was actively and voluntarily engaged in enlightening rural men against leading lazy, unproductive lives of gambling and drinking. Pak Hyon-suk also was very active in social work on behalf of destitute women, teaching them occupational skills.

The propagation of Christianity in Korea was especially significant for women because of its idea of equality between men and women before God. Also, Protestant missionary work enlightened women by providing them with formal education and with opportunities to assume roles outside the family.[28] Pioneer political women like Pak Hyon-suk, Pak Sun-ch'on, and Yim Yong-sin all attended Christian missionary schools, became teachers, and got involved in the Independence Movement. Christian influences, coupled with the oppressive political conditions, had revolutionary effects on their lives.

These women legislators of the pioneer generation, however, should not be regarded as "political Christians." Unlike some male politicians who made their way to Christian churches with stronger political motivations than religious needs, it seemed that pioneer political women embraced the doctrine of Christianity wholeheartedly.

For example, Yim Yong-sin, coming from a well-to-do gentry family, at first found it demeaning that she should clean her room and perform other menial work herself at the school dormitory. But she soon came to accept the Protestant work ethic as a result of her life at a missionary school. When she went home during a summer vacation, she tried to change the attitude of the villagers toward work by her own example, which astounded them. When she went to the United States to study, she did not depend on her brothers financially. Instead, she worked and saved enough money to go to school. She took all kinds of jobs in order to be financially independent, at first working as a housekeeper, gardener, and maid, and later giving lectures on Oriental history; she also worked at Korean churches, sold farm produce, ran a gas station, and leased trucks. She was able to save $10,000 during her first two years in the United States. The money she saved and brought back to Korea enabled her to start her own school, Chungang, which became the first private college founded by a Korean woman.[29]

Numerous episodes in these women's lives indicate that for them, Christian religion was a constant source of spiritual renewal and gave them an abiding conviction that justice would prevail. Their predispositions of willfulness and indomitable courage to seek truth and justice seem to have been reinforced, if not engendered, by their life experiences and religious faith. Pak Hyon-suk endeavored to enlighten President Park Chung Hee and others of the power elite who were not religious on "the existence of God, the necessity of religious faith and its special taste" during her second legislative tenure.[30] It was she who initiated and headed the President's Breakfast Prayer Association in the National Assembly in 1966.

Although religious faith seems to have played a significant part in the achievements of professional careers in public life, it had remarkably little impact on gender-role attitudes of progressive Christian women of this study in their private lives, as described earlier in this chapter. Perhaps the doctrine of the trinity (the Father, the Son, and the Holy Ghost) in the cultural context of male-dominated Korean society has had the effect of sanctifying the father-son alignment of patrilineality, which is the backbone of Korean society. Furthermore, Christianity, despite its concept of egalitarianism before God, basically upholds patriarchal values and attitudes concerning gender roles of married couples, as underscored by various stories in the Bible. Hence it is not surprising that these women's beliefs in Christianity have not contributed to the transformation of traditional gender-role attitudes in their private lives. In this regard, it is noteworthy that a recent sociological study on gender-role attitudes in the United States concluded that "church attendance and a fundamentalist Protestant religious identification tend to preserve more traditional outlooks."[31]

PERSONALITY

Yim Yong-sin once stated in an interview that "eighty percent of a person's character can be cultivated while twenty percent of it is inborn."[32] Putting aside the question of whether personality traits of the informants are inborn or cultivated, various episodes in life histories of elected women lawmakers underscore the strength of *kojib* (stubbornness) and its crucial role in bringing about turning points in their lives.

Yim Yong-sin, for example, eagerly wanted to go to school, yet her father was adamantly opposed to the idea of a girl receiving formal education. Any girl with less determination than Yim Yong-sin would have become sadly resigned to her fate. Yong-sin, however, staged a hunger strike, which forced her father to yield on the fourth day when Yong-sin became so weak as to be almost unconscious. Her willfulness won her the precious opportunity to receive education, which made a world of difference not only for her own life but also for her family and her country.

The biography of Pak Hyon-suk states that she was "a very stubborn child even though she was neither the firstborn nor the youngest one."[33] Her continuous involvement in the resistance movement after the March First 1919 Independence Movement resulted in harsh torture and imprisonment. Pak Hyon-suk was incarcerated three times, for over four years in total, for her anti-Japanese activities during the two and a half decades after the March First Movement until the Liberation. But with a sense of justice, courage, and strong determination, she never ceased her loyal commitment to fight for national independence.

Pak Sun-ch'on also demonstrated her willfulness by defying her father's decision to marry her off at an early age. As president of the Korea Women's Association, Pak Sun-ch'on defied President Rhee with her bold announcement that her organization would maintain political neutrality until the day of national unification and would not join the Liberal Party that President Rhee created. Her stubbornness, sense of justice, and courage led her to confront the revered, powerful President Rhee, a move that marked a turning point not only in their relationship as fellow patriots but also in her political career. From then on, she belonged to the opposition party and was one of its leading figures until her death (see Chapter 5 for more details).

Kim Ch'ol-an told me that she was determined to participate in socio-political activities, even though she knew she had to postpone her personal plans for many years after her marriage. Her election campaign anecdotes and Korean War episodes amply attest to her strong determination and courage (see Chapter 5).

The second-generation elected assemblywomen have also demonstrated a strong determination and a great deal of tenacity, courage, and oratorical talents. Kim Ok-son was so determined to assume the family headship (in place of her lost brother) and to lead a public life that she chose to renounce her female identity when confronted with severe criticism by conservative people of Ch'ungch'ong province for transcending the conventional division of gender roles. Her sense of justice and the extent of her courage were crystallized in her criticism of the dictatorship of the

Park regime during her speech in the National Assembly in 1975. She was forced to stop her speech, and the ire of President Park and the ruling party officials resulted in her resignation from the National Assembly. The incident was referred to as "Kim Ok-son *p'adong* (crisis)."[34] (Chapter 7 presents more details of the incident and its devastating effect on the political career of Kim Ok-son.)

As for Kim Yun-dok, her various wartime experiences of cruelty and conflict sharply fostered her sense of justice and desire to participate actively in politics so that she could help bring about a better world to live in. Her strong determination and a supportive husband made it possible for her—a mother of three young children at the time of matriculation—to go back to college to study law in the early 1960s, when married women in college were a rare phenomenon in Korea.

For Kim Chong-rye, her personal experience of poverty and her empathy for the financial sufferings of poor peasant neighbors made her determine to devote her life to enlightening rural people and improving their living conditions. Her active involvement in community work and refusal to get married alienated her parents, who disowned her for some time. She had to live at the home of one of her classmates for several months before she moved to Seoul. Her sense of justice and courage led her to become one of the first people to denounce the military for taking over the government unlawfully. She was arrested on a sedition charge and imprisoned for three years under the Park regime.

British Prime Minister Margaret Thatcher—who is described as having "an inexorable will"—remarked in an interview that politicians' "difference is in personality, far from the differences between the male and female in the issues that I have to deal with."[35] She also stated that flair, hard work, and vitality were necessary ingredients for her success.

It is noteworthy that the traits that made Thatcher "a success story of modern times"—determination, tenacity, disdain of compromise, and "guts" —are strikingly similar to those of elected women legislators of this study. They also seemed to have been gifted with a wealth of inherent vitality, which they used in their hard work with a sense of mission. Further, the life histories of these women legislators suggest that harsh personal experiences under the particular social and political circumstances of the country reinforced some of the most salient personality traits they share, such as stubbornness or willfulness, a strong sense of mission, and abundant courage. For instance, all the elected women legislators, except Kim Yun-dok, had been imprisoned for their political activities, and perhaps they all felt the same fortifying effect of imprisonment on their determination to pursue a political career, as Kim Ok-son stated during her interview.

NOTES

1. Kirkpatrick (1974).
2. Werner (1966).
3. Darcy and Song (1986:677) report that "only slightly more than half" of their women sample were married.
4. Personal communication, while in the field, with Cho Hyejong.
5. Kirkpatrick (1974); Lynn (1979:417); and Vallance (1979:67).
6. SPC (1968).
7. See K. Lee (1984:360) for a "movement to buy Korean" in the 1920s.
8. SPC (1968).
9. T. Yi (1986); C. Yim (1985).
10. Pak (1974-75).
11. For more details on the student meeting, see K. Lee (1984:341).
12. Son (1972:310) reports the name as Han Sun-kyo, while two other sources (PCC 1959:146; Yim 1951:202) record it as Han Su-kyo.
13. Son (1972:309-14).
14. Yim Ch'ol-sun became a legislator in 1981 and was reelected to the twelfth National Assembly.
15. The term *hyonji-ch'o* (the local wife) came into use initially to refer to the woman cohabiting with a Japanese businessman (or sometimes a male Korean resident in Japan) who commutes between Korea and Japan on business.
16. Thornton, Duane, and Camburn (1983:225).
17. Kammeyer (1966).
18. *Han'guk Ilbo*, June 9, 1968.
19. Smolowe (1989).
20. KWDI (1985).
21. Son (1972:256).
22. The autobiography of Helen Kim (1965) reveals a similar story of miraculous recovery from a serious illness by the strength of her faith in God.
23. Darcy and Song (1986:675) also noted the Christian predominance among political women of their study.
24. *Han'guk Ilbo*, January 19, 1986.
25. For discussions of the impact of Japanese rule on Korean Christianity, see Chung (1961); Clark (1986:8-14); Henderson (1968); and Kang (1986; 1987).
26. Henderson (1968:208). However, Oliver (1954) portrays Syngman Rhee as a devout Christian rather than a "political Christian."
27. Henderson (1968:208).
28. H. Lee (1977).
29. Son (1972:251-281).

30. SPC (1968:444).
31. Thornton, Duane, and Camburn (1983:211).
32. Son (1972:649).
33. SPC (1968:20).
34. O. Kim (1984); Om (1986).
35. Michael (1986).

5

Pathways to the National Assembly

Korean women began to participate in public life during the so-called enlightenment period (1876-1910) by attending church functions, receiving formal education at school, and organizing associations for women.[1] Enlightenment activities reached their height during the first decade of the twentieth century, when Korea began to lose its sovereignty and came under Japanese control. Under the shadow of impending doom, progressive intellectuals rushed to found more schools for women, believing that the education of women, as teachers of children, was even more important than men's.[2]

The pioneer generation of women politicians came from the ranks of Christian women who were educated during the Japanese colonization of Korea (1910-45). They found their first opportunities to be directly involved in political activities during the March First Movement in 1919. They were pulled into the resistance movement against the Japanese. The process of the emergence of political women in modern Korea, therefore, is best understood in the context of the larger process of the resistance against Japanese rule, especially the March First Movement (Samil Undong) of 1919, which proved to be the turning point in the lives of the women legislators of the pioneer generation.

The March First Movement epitomized the animosity of the Korean people toward the Japanese colonizers and the yearning of the Koreans for national independence. It remains one of the most significant social movements in Korean history, in that grass-roots political sentiments were expressed contemporaneously across the country in a nonviolent fashion. Particularly noteworthy is that female students and young women actively participated in the March First Movement. Of the 471 women arrested by the colonial police for their participation in the movement, 311 were under the age of twenty-five, and 218 women were either students or teachers.[3]

For the first time in Korean history, nonroyal women took their place on the national political stage. Women's formal education, the oppressive politics of the colonial government, and Christian conviction that justice will prevail were some of the major factors that contributed to the appearance of women as leaders and participants in the March First Movement. The point is conspicuously manifested in the life histories of some of my main sample who courageously participated in the movement.

WOMEN'S ELECTORAL HISTORY

The three women legislators of the pioneer generation, Yim Yong-sin (1899-1977), Pak Sun-ch'on (1898-1982), and Pak Hyon-suk (1896-1980), were working as teachers before their active participation in the March First Movement, as leaders of the demonstration marches in Chonju, Masan, and P'yongyang, respectively. They all experienced imprisonment due to their participation in the independence movement. They continued their participation in the resistance, risking their lives to help bring liberation of the country from Japanese rule. After liberation, they were appointed to high office in the Rhee government and were elected to the National Assembly.

So far, the greatest number of women candidates—excluding those for the national constituency—ran for legislative seats in the first general election held in May, 1948. Eighteen women, including Pak Sun-ch'on and Kim Ch'ol-an, competed in the National Assembly election, but none of them won.[4] Yim Yong-sin was still in the United States on her diplomatic mission (see the following section).

Thus, when the first National Assembly convened on May 31, 1948, it was an exclusively male gathering. Hwang Ae-dok and Hwang Hyon-suk, two among the eighteen women candidates, later ran again when special elections were held to fill the vacancies created by President Rhee in October, 1948, and Ambassador Chang Myon in March, 1949. They both lost the elections again. Only Yim Yong-sin was able to garner a victory in the special election held in Andong in January, 1949, to fill a vacancy left by Chong Hyon-mo upon his appointment to the office of the governor of North Kyongsang province. Yim Yong-sin thus became the first woman lawmaker in Korea and the only female member of the first National Assembly. Pak Sun-ch'on in the meantime was appointed to the Board of Inspection by President Rhee.

The experiences in the first general election must have discouraged many women from seeking a place in the National Assembly, for the number of women candidates dropped to eleven in the second general election, which included Yim Yong-sin and Pak Sun-ch'on as legislators.

The results of the first two general elections suggest that Korean voters were not generally prepared to allow female participation in the National Assembly, but they were willing to make exceptions for outstanding female candidates such as Yim Yong-sin and Pak Sun-ch'on, who had already proven their political skills and leadership in the March First Movement of 1919 and in the Rhee administration as high officials.

By the time the third general election took place in 1954, the political climate had substantially changed. President Rhee created the Liberal Party, and more than half of the members of the third National Assembly belonged to it, in contrast to the dominance of the independents (60 percent) in the second National Assembly. Pak Sun-ch'on, who refused to join the Liberal Party and ran as an independent, failed to win the election. Yim Yong-sin, who had run for the vice-presidency without success in 1952, also lost the election to Yu Chin-san, a leading politician in the opposition camp, by 14,306 to 15,596,[5] and returned to her educational career at Chungang University (which she had founded). A new female face, Kim Ch'ol-an (a forty-two-year-old housewife whose father-in-law and husband strongly supported her participation in political life) showed up in the third National Assembly.

In contrast to the third National Assembly, where Kim Ch'ol-an was the only female member, the fourth National Assembly had three elected female lawmakers (Kim Ch'ol-an, Pak Sun-ch'on, and Pak Hyon-suk), the greatest number of elected women legislators the National Assembly has had in its thirteen-term history.

Then the presidential election held in March, 1960, precipitated the demise of the First Republic. President Rhee, at the age of eighty-five, ran for his fourth term, with Yi Ki-bung as his running mate. Yim Yong-sin believed that Yi Ki-bung was not a worthy candidate and that nobody could better assist the elderly President than she. She decided to compete for the vice-presidential election, despite heavy pressure and sharp criticism from the Liberal Party and the Korea Women's Association (which was headed by Pak Maria, wife of the vice-presidential candidate Yi Ki-bung). In the meantime, the opposition presidential candidate Cho Pyong-ok went to the United States to undergo surgery and died there. Thus, President Rhee was reelected unopposed, but the election of vice-presidential candidate Yi Ki-bung was so rigged that Yim Yong-sin received not a single vote in the Huksok-dong district where she and many of her supporters resided.[6]

Student-led mass demonstrations protesting election frauds resulted in a sudden finale to the Rhee regime in April, 1960. The opposition Democratic Party came into power in August, 1960, and enjoyed the status of ruling party for a brief period until it was overthrown by the military coup of May, 1961.

College students and military establishments are the two elements of Korean society that have most profoundly influenced contemporary politics.[7] After the student uprising brought down the First Republic

(1948-60), some students ran for legislative seats in the fifth National Assembly election in 1960, but none were elected.[8]   Then the military revolution of May, 1961, ushered in a new phase in the political history of the nation.

When the military ascended to power with the establishment of the Third Republic in 1963, there were no female members in the cabinet of President Park Chung Hee. In fact, during the eighteen-year rule of the Park regime, there were no women officials at the cabinet level, nor were there any elected female lawmakers from the ruling party. The presidency and several important cabinet positions continued to be occupied by former military men. This phase of Korean politics, which began with the founding of the Third Republic in 1963, has been described as "quasi-civilianization"[9] or "civilitary" government.[10]

The military revolution of 1961 was an important watershed in the history of modern Korea. Since then, political power has been anchored in the group of former military leaders. The scope and variety of military roles in contemporary Korea is such that

it is difficult fully to comprehend . . . the cumulative impact of the process by which millions of Koreans have been exposed to military institutions and military ideas. . . . [T]he social, economic, and political changes stimulated directly or indirectly by the military have been more far-reaching and significant than those generated by any other single group within the society.[11]

In a society where military careers have become an important means of access to the political power structure, women with political aspirations are automatically placed in a greatly disadvantageous position, as they do not hold the credentials of military experience that could enhance their political profiles.

With the military revolution came the end of the era of the pioneering generation of political women whose experiences within the resistance movement served as prestigious credentials for their legislative careers. In fact, one effect of the military coup was the "changeover of the generations."[12] The time had also come for a generational transition among political women.

Each decade in the postrevolution era has witnessed a new kind of elected female legislator. The 1960s saw a young woman wearing men's clothes win a legislative seat after going through a tedious legal battle against election fraud. Kim Ok-son won the year-long legal battle in 1968 to become the first elected *ch'onyo* (unmarried, literally virgin) legislator of the National Assembly. She was thirty-three years old at the time of the 1967 election.

The decade of the 1970s also witnessed politically significant events, both domestic and international, for women. In 1973, Kim Yun-dok, a housewife with six children and a supportive husband, won a parliamentary election in the Cholla province. The United Nations' declaration of the Decade for Women in 1975 legitimated serious discussions of women's issues in the male-dominated society. The proportional party list system allowed the political participation of a greater number of the second-generation women as appointive members of the National Assembly. Within the decade of the 1970s, twenty-two legislative seats were allotted to nineteen women (three of whom served for two terms). Among them were women holding Ph.D.'s in political science, as well as leaders of women's organizations who knew little about national politics.

With the establishment of the Fifth Republic in 1981, Kim Chong-rye, a longtime activist who used to be regarded as a dyed-in-the-wool oppositionist, won a legislative seat in the eleventh general election as a member of the ruling Democratic Justice Party. Eight other women joined the legislative body as appointed members. The twelfth National Assembly had two elected female members (Kim Ok-sun and Kim Chong-rye) and six appointed assemblywomen, one of whom soon resigned. The thirteenth National Assembly had six appointed women members but no elected woman legislator. The fourteenth National Assembly again has no elected woman legislator and has two less appointed women members than the thirteenth (see Tables 5.1 and 5.2).

The number of women legislators has increased considerably since the military revolution. Forty-two women joined the legislature for the first time between 1963 and 1992. However, only three of them (Kim Ok-son, Kim Yun-dok, and Kim Chong-rye)[13] were elected to the National Assembly by popular vote. Therefore, an overwhelming majority of the women legislators of the postrevolution era became members of the National Assembly due to the proportional party list system. Most of them ultimately owed their legislative careers to final approval of their appointments by Presidents Park, Chun, or Roh. Their legislative appointments are discussed in the following chapter.

WOMEN LEGISLATORS AND PRESIDENTS

Although no woman legislator in Korea achieved her position by dint of her kin relations to a male politician, that did not mean male politicians had no role to play in the career development of political women. On the contrary, the influence of male politicians, especially that of the presidents, was an important factor in the careers of Korean women legislators.

Table 5.1
Elected Legislators in South Korea (1st to 14th National Assembly)

	National Assembly		M.E.L.* Number	F.E.L.** Name
P	1st	(1948-50)	199	Yim Yong-sin
R				
E	2nd	(1950-54)	208	Pak Sun-ch'on
R				Yim Yong-sin
E				
V	3rd	(1954-58)	202	Kim Ch'ol-an
O				
L	4th	(1958-60)	230	Kim Ch'ol-an
U				Pak Hyon-suk
T				Pak Sun-ch'on
I				
O	5th	(1960-61)	232	Pak Sun-ch'on
N				

Military Rule (1961-1963)

	National Assembly		M.E.L.* Number	F.E.L.** Name
P	6th	(1963-67)	130	Pak Sun-ch'on
O				
S	7th	(1967-71)	130	Kim Ok-son
T				
R	8th	(1971-72)	153	---
E				
V	9th	(1973-79)	144	Kim Ok-son
O				Kim Yun-dok
L				
U	10th	(1979-80)	153	Kim Yun-dok
T				
I	11th	(1981-85)	183	Kim Chong-rye
O				
N	12th	(1985-88)	182	Kim Chong-rye
				Kim Ok-son
	13th	(1988-92)	224	---
	14th	(1992-)	237	---

*male elected legislators
**female elected legislators

Table 5.2
Appointed Legislators in South Korea (6th to 14th National Assembly)

National Assembly	M.A.L.* Number	Female Appointed Legislators Number and Name	
6th (1963-67)	43	1 Pak Hyon-suk	
7th (1967-71)	42	2 Pak Sun-ch'on	
		Yi Mary	
8th (1971-72)	46	5 Kim Hyon-suk	
		Kim Ok-ja	
		Kim Yun-dok	
		Mo Yun-suk	
		P'yon Chong-hi	
9th (1973-79)	63	10 Chong Pok-hyang	So Yong-hi
		Ho Mu-in	Yi Pom-jun
		Kim Ok-ja	Yi Suk-chong
		Ku Im-hoe	Yi Sung-bok
		Pak Chong-ja	Yun Yo-hun
10th (1979-80)	70	7 Hyon Ki-sun	Sin Tong-sun
		Kim Ok-yol	So Yong-hi
		Kim Yong-ja	Yun Yo-hun
		Pak Hyon-so	
11th (1981-85)	84	8 Hwang San-song	Kim Mo-im
		Mun Yong-ju	Yi Kyong-suk
		Kim Haeng-ja	Yi Yong-hi
		Kim Hyon-ja	Yi Yun-ja
12th (1985-88)	86	6 Han Yang-sun	Kim Yong-jong
		Kim Chang-suk	Pak Hye-kyong
		Kim Hyon-ja	Yang Kyung-ja
13th (1988-92)	69	6 Kim Chang-suk	To Yong-sim
		Pak Yong-suk	Yang Kyong-ja
		Sin Yong-sun	Yi Yun-ja
14th (1992-)	58	4 Chu Yang-ja	
		Kang Pu-ja	
		Kang Son-yong	
		Yi U-jong	

*male appointed legislators

For example, President Rhee——who appointed more women to high government office than did any other Korean president——exerted an inordinate degree of decisive influence on the professional lives of the pioneer women politicians in one way or another.[14]

In the case of Yim Yong-sin, her close relationship with President Rhee was instrumental in her political career, especially during the earlier part of the Rhee government. Yim Yong-sin's acquaintance with Rhee dated back more than two decades before he became the first president of the Republic of Korea in 1948. She even received an indirect marriage proposal from Syngman Rhee through a pastor during her visit to Washington, D.C., after her graduation from the University of Southern California in 1931.[15] Her brothers, however, objected to her marrying Rhee because he had an estranged wife in Korea and they thought he was too old for their sister. Rhee was twenty-four years older than Yim.

When Syngman Rhee returned to Korea on October 16, 1945, after thirty-three years of political exile abroad, Yim Yong-sin devoted herself to giving him whatever assistance she could render. In addition to being a fellow independence fighter, she performed "the work of wife, secretary, and housekeeper" for him, who apprarently regarded her as a "daughter."[16] She shared the same roof with Rhee until the return of his wife in March of the next year. Some people were jealous of her intimate relationship with Rhee and suspicious rumors spread as to their relationship.[17]

When the Representative Democratic Council of South Korea came into being in February, 1946, Rhee, as the chairman, appointed Yim as his secretary, to the amazement of his more conservative male colleagues. Six months later, in August, 1946, Yim was designated by Rhee as the official delegate of the Representative Democratic Council so that she could be dispatched to the United States on a critical diplomatic mission. Some male members expressed their "absolute opposition" to the idea of sending a woman as the representative of Korea.[18] The Council, however, gave unanimous approval after Chairman Rhee pointed out why he thought Yim was the best choice to persuade the Washington government and to make appeals to the United Nations for Korean independence. He stated that this difficult task could be entrusted only to someone who well knew the Americans and their way of life. Yim had studied in the United States, where she had resided for more than a decade. Yim had also been befriended by many influential people in America who helped her finance Chungang College, which she founded in Seoul. They could be of assistance to her in this important diplomatic mission.

When Yim left for the United States on September 1, 1946, she became the first woman in Korean history to be sent abroad to represent a political organization. With strong determination and assertive tenacity, she worked hard to accomplish her diplomatic mission.[19] The United States submitted the Korean issue to the United Nations, and the General Assembly of the United Nations voted for the resolution for the independence of Korea on November 14, 1947.

Soon the U.N. Temporary Commission on Korea was formed.[20] The Commission arrived in Seoul on January 8, 1948. Initially, Ambassador K. P. S. Menon of India, the chairman, considered that a coalition government between North and South Korea under the leadership of Kim Ku or Kim Kyu-sik should be established in Korea.[21]

Two women had a major influence in changing Menon's opinion on the Korean political situation, thereby helping Rhee to achieve his political goal.[22] Mo Yun-suk (who later became an appointed member of the National Assembly) played her role on the informal, domestic scene, while Yim Yong-sin as the national representative played her role on the formal, international stage.

When Mo Yun-suk (1909-90), a well-known poet, was introduced to Menon during his official visit to Korea as the head of the U.N. Commission,[23] they were able to strike up a friendly relationship owing to their common interest in Indian poetry. Rhee noticed this and asked Mo's help in bringing Menon to his residence. On the eve of his departure, Menon received a phone call from Mo, who suggested a ride to Kumgok-nung to enjoy the snowy landscape. Menon accepted the invitation and rode in a car with Mo. As instructed by Mo, the driver, however, took them to Rhee's house instead of to the royal tomb in Kumgok. Menon had not much choice but to behave diplomatically. He met with Rhee over tea and heard his political viewpoints and pleas for national independence until the wee hours of the morning. In the car returning to his hotel, Mo handed Menon a petition scroll given to her by Rhee. It contained a thousand signatures that endorsed the establishment of the Korean government and the election of Rhee as its president.[24]

Upon Menon's return to the United Nations, Yim Yong-sin invited him to dinner and explained the political situation in Korea. She pleaded to him on behalf of Syngman Rhee and delivered to him Rhee's plan. The final report Menon submitted to the United Nations was in favor of the establishment of a Korean government under the leadership of Syngman Rhee. He attached to his report the scroll he received from Mo as supporting material.[25] Based on the report, the U.N. Interim Assembly passed a resolution on February 26, 1948, ordering the U.N. Commission on Korea to conduct elections, even if those elections could only be held in South Korea. Yim wrote in her autobiography: "We had won, but at what a cost. We had won a government, but the country was divided."[26]

After the general election, Rhee was elected the president of the Republic of Korea. President Rhee now had to express his gratitude to the two women. To the surprise of the nation, the president appointed Yim

Yong-sin to be the minister of commerce and industry. She was the only female member of his cabinet. The grateful president praised Yim Yong-sin for her distinguished services to the country in his inaugural speech, although his secretary had advised him not to single out any individual's name on such a formal occasion as the inaugural ceremony. President Rhee further stated that her efforts would be forever remembered in conjuction with the establishment of the Republic of Korea.[27]

As for Mo Yun-suk, she was given the honor of officially representing Korea at the U.N. General Meeting in Paris in the fall of 1948. Besides Mo, the Korean delegation included such political figures as Chang Myon (who was elected vice-president in 1956 and became the prime minister in 1960), Cho Pyong-ok (a presidential candidate in 1960), Yim Yong-sin, and Helen Kim (the first Korean woman to earn a Ph.D. and president of Ewha Women's University).[28] On December 12, 1948, the delegation obtained official U.N. recognition that the Republic of Korea was the only legitimate government on the Korean peninsula. More than two decades later, Mo Yun-suk was appointed to the eighth National Assembly by President Park Chung Hee, which, Mo Yun-suk said on the phone, was probably due to a recognition of her "civilian diplomacy."

Pak Sun-ch'on's autobiographical essay reveals that Syngman Rhee wanted her to give up her candidacy in the Chongno-kap district in Seoul during the first general election so that his friend Yi Yun-yong could win the race. Pak Sun-ch'on flatly refused to relinquish her constituency, and in her first campaign speech, she vehemently criticized Rhee for his presumptuous and authoritarian attitude. Pak Sun-ch'on lost the race to Yi Yun-yong, who was Rhee's first choice for prime minister but was rejected by the National Assembly[29] and who was later appointed minister of social affairs.[30] According to Pak Sun-ch'on, President Syngman Rhee expressed his regrets to her and soon appointed her and Pak Hyon-suk to the Board of Inspection.[31]

However, when President Rhee urged all staff members of major national voluntary associations to join the Liberal Party he created in 1951, Pak Sun-ch'on, as president of the Korea Women's Association, boldly announced that her organization would maintain political neutrality until the day of national unification. Her visit to the office of President Rhee on December 24, 1953, marked the end of their cordial relationship as fellow independence fighters and patriots. The government began to exert oppressive pressures on her organization. The minister of home affairs openly declared that as long as Pak Sun-ch'on headed the association, the government would withhold its subsidy to the organization.[32] She resigned from the post and ran as an independent in the May 1954 election, but was not returned to the third National Assembly. Soon she joined in the formation of the Democratic Party (Minjudang)[33] and remained a leading figure in the major opposition party, even assuming its leadership from July 1963 to February 1967 (see Chapter 8).

For Kim Ch'ol-an, opportunities to meet and work for President Rhee came during the Korean War years. She said she went to the front in Yongch'on dressed in military attire and to P'yongyang to observe the war situation at the request of President Rhee. When the war was over, she won the 1954 election, endorsed by the Liberal Party.

Pak Hyon-suk also benefited from her cordial relationship with Syngman Rhee in her political career. After her escape from Pyongyang to Seoul in February, 1946, she was asked by Rhee to head the Women's Bureau in the National Unification Headquarters (Minjok T'ongil Ch'ongbonbu). In November, 1946, she was appointed to the South Korean Interim Legislative Assembly. The next year she was nominated to the Central Commission for Election Management. After the establishment of the Republic of Korea, she was appointed by President Rhee to his cabinet as minister without portfolio in 1952. Six years later in 1958, she ran for a legislative seat with an endorsement of the ruling Liberal Party and won.

Presidential influence was not necessarily so beneficial for the second-generation elected women legislators as it had been for the pioneer-generation women legislators.

In the case of Kim Ok-son, she was forced out of the political arena for offending President Park with her critical speech on the dictatorial government, and suffered harsh political persecution as long as President Park lived (see Chapter 7). The legislative career of Kim Yun-dok is uniquely devoid of any direct presidential influence. In contrast, Kim Chong-rye experienced both negative and positive effects of presidential power in her political career.

Kim Chong-rye, the latest addition to the tiny pool of the elected women legislators, began her involvement in political life right after liberation. In comparison to the younger Kim Ok-son and Kim Yun-dok, Kim Chong-rye was very deeply affected by the postliberation political chaos under U.S. military rule. She obtained her political socialization firsthand by devoting herself to rural enlightenment work in her home town of Tamyang in Cholla province during this period, and later by working for national youth organizations.

Kim Chong-rye feels particularly indebted to General Yi Pom-sok, an independence fighter and the first prime minister of the First Republic. Under his tutelage she joined the Liberal Party as a Central Committee member at the age of twenty-five. When Yi's political clout was crushed by President Rhee, Kim Chong-rye also left the Liberal Party. She told me that she was like his adopted daughter, so that when she received a subsequent offer from Pak Maria to rejoin the Liberal Party, she initially refused out of her sense of loyalty to Yi Pom-sok.

During the interview, Kim Chong-rye stated that she was the first to publicly denounce the military for their "political burglary." She was arrested for her involvement in an "antirevolution incident" and was imprisoned for three years. She was one of the many politicians who were placed under the restraint of the Political Purification Law. When the ban on her political activities was finally lifted in 1969, she formed the Korean League of Women Voters [Han'guk Yosong Yukwonja Yonmaeng] and was working as the founding chair of the League when she first met General Chun Doo Hwan during the Kwangju revolt. She said she was called to an interview with General Chun Doo Hwan during the violent street demonstrations in Kwangju (capital of South Cholla), which turned into a riot by mid-May of 1980 (see Chapter 1). As a native of Cholla Province, Kim Chong-rye was deeply concerned about the unrest and went to the city with Yi T'ae-yong (the first woman lawyer in Korea) to do whatever she could. Kim Chong-rye said she had another meeting with General Chun at her request in order to discuss the tragic situation with him.

It is obvious that she impressed General Chun during their meetings, for she was soon invited to join the power elite in their endeavors to forge "a new era" in Korean society. It was a difficult decision, for she had been associated with dissident forces since the early days of the Park regime. Seeking advice from her *sonbae* (seniors) she agonized over the decision for a month. She came to the conclusion that both the ruling and the opposition camps were riding the same "boat named Korea," and that at this critical crossroads in national history it would be an act of arrogance for her to refuse to join in steering the boat out of a maelstrom.

Kim Chong-rye said that her meeting with General Chun Doo Hwan over the Kwangju revolt in May, 1980, brought about a turning point in her political career. In October, 1980, she was appointed to the Legislative Council for National Safeguarding (Kukka Powi Ippop Hoeui) by President Chun (see Chapter 1). She then joined the Democratic Justice Party when it was created in January, 1981, and won the election for the eleventh National Assembly.

Kim Chong-rye, whose political career had been devastated under the rule of President Park because of her involvement in anti-military government activities, thus was able to launch into legislative life due to the staunch personal support of President Chun Doo Hwan. She also served in the cabinet of President Chun Doo Hwan from 1982 to 1985. Kim Chong-rye was reelected to the twelfth National Assembly but failed to win the thirteenth general election under the new constitution of the Sixth Republic (see Chapter 6).

Kim Chong-rye's entry into the legislature as a member of the ruling Democratic Justice Party (which was founded by a group of former military men) was a great surprise to many of her friends and acquaintances because she had been associated with dissident forces since the early days of the Park regime. The process of the career development for Kim Chong-rye and many other women legislators of this study underlines the power of the chief executive in affecting the courses of personal lives of individuals, especially in an authoritarian culture.

Various studies of Korean society and politics have presented authoritarianism as the most salient feature of Korean political culture.[34] The Rhee regime operated on the "personalistic authority" of Syngman Rhee, while the governments after the military coup have been described as "militaristic" authoritarian regimes.[35] In the authoritarian political system, where decision-making power is concentrated in the office of the president, it is not surprising that the influence of Presidents Rhee, Park, and Chun was undeniably strong in the career courses of almost all women legislators.

The strength of presidential influence in the lives of women politicians is a reflection of the political history of the authoritarian regimes that have ruled the nation. But the mosaic of presidential influence seems to mirror the basic differences in the values and attitudes of each president toward women's roles in politics.

Syngman Rhee had earned a Ph.D. in political science at Princeton University and lived abroad as a political exile for more than three decades before he returned to Korea in 1945 after liberation. Robert Oliver, who had worked closely with Syngman Rhee in Washington before the liberation of Korea from the Japanese and frequently in Korea after liberation, called him an archetype of that "new man" who attained the inner integration of the cultures of the East and West and asserted that Syngman Rhee was among the few Asian leaders to foster a significant movement for feminist rights in the Orient.[36] Rhee's first speech upon his return home seemed to support what Oliver wrote. Rhee exhorted men and women to unite in their efforts for national independence.[37] Also, during the first half of the Rhee regime, more women were appointed to high office than under any other president.[38]

By the latter part of the Rhee government, however, his good relationships with women politicians seemed to have evaporated. It has often been suggested that the Austrian born wife of President Rhee was to blame for the loss of the close working relationships between the president and the pioneer women politicians. Mo Yun-suk wrote that Madam Rhee was overly protective of her husband and intimated that it was her jealousy of the women followers—whose loyal assistance was invaluable to his political success—that caused the demise of the cordial contacts between President Rhee and women politicians and supporters.[39]

Indeed, Yim Yong-sin no longer seemed to enjoy a close relationship with President Rhee by the time she ran for vice-president in 1952. And when Yim Yong-sin ran again as a vice-presidential candidate upholding Syngman Rhee as president in the 1960 presidential election, President Rhee chose Yi Ki-bung of the Liberal Party as his running mate. The protective wall surrounding President Rhee was such that Yim Yong-sin had to force her way into his office on the night of April 20, 1960, to inform him of the gravity of the student demonstrations and advise him to resign.[40]

In contrast to the Rhee government, what is noteworthy about the Park administration with regard to women legislators is that there was *no elected female legislator from the ruling party*: the two elected assemblywomen (Kim Ok-son and Kim Yun-dok) both belonged to the opposition camp. Also, during his eighteen-year rule, President Park Chung Hee never recruited a woman into his cabinet. The majority of women President Park chose to appoint to the legislature were women in "feminine" occupations who had no personal aspiration to be politically active.

Born and raised in a conservative rural village in Kyongsang province, Park Chung Hee was a professional military man whose values and attitudes concerning gender roles seemed unmistakably traditional. He was a "distinctly Asian" leader whose socialization contained no substantial element of Westernization.[41]

Likewise, President Chun, who also came from a rural village in Kyongsang province,[42] had been a professional military man and had little Western influence in his socialization. Yet, the difference in age and perhaps his eagerness to enhance his administration's public image as the "new era" may have influenced Chun Doo Hwan to lend strong support to a woman activist—Kim Chong-rye—by inviting her to join the ruling party, endorsing her candidacy for the legislature and even recruiting her into his cabinet.

DYNAMICS OF GENDER-ROLE CHANGE

Had it not been for the independence movement, the emergence of the pioneering generation of women politicians in Korea might have been much more difficult and long delayed. The patterns of career development of pioneer women politicians demonstrate the importance of sociohistorical circumstances in bringing about significant changes in attitudes concerning gender roles.

The analysis of life histories of elected women legislators suggests that a state of liminality in political life is a social condition that is conducive to women's active participation in politics. A state of liminality, which Turner discussed in his study of rituals, is characterized by *communitas* or fellowship, equality, absence of rank, minimization of sex distinctions, and unselfishness.[43] A most conspicuous example of the state of liminality in Korean political life occurred under Japanese colonial rule, which helped produce the pioneering generation of women legislators in modern Korea.

Under Japanese colonial rule, especially during its first decade, which obliterated Korean men's power in political life,[44] men and women were equal in their powerlessness in the political arena and found themselves in a state of liminality in political life. The traditional sexual apartheid based on the strict Confucian gender-role ideology was lifted during the Japanese rule, particularly within the Christian community (see Chapter 4 for a discussion of the role of Christianity in the modernization movement in Korea). In the urgent struggle for national salvation from the enemy, the Confucian ideology of male superiority was replaced by Christian egalitarianism, at least until national independence was won. Korean women were not only welcomed as participants, but some of them were entrusted with leadership positions in the March First Movement, a political event that occurred during a most notable state of liminality in Korean politics. Thus, those particular historical circumstances allowed Korean women to plunge directly into national politics without going through the lengthy struggles of the suffragist movement common in the West, Japan, and many nations in the Third World.[45]

After liberation, women who had fought for independence continued their active involvement in national politics. During the thirteen general elections since liberation, the highest number of women candidates vied for an elective seat of the National Assembly at the first general election in 1948, when the nation was making a great political transition from a Japanese colony to an independent democratic nation. Once the government of the Republic of Korea began to take root, the political climate turned discouraging to female participation. Except for a few exceptional cases, women were pushed back into the domain of traditional women's work.

This pattern of women's political participation suggests that a period of major political transition generates a state of liminality, which encourages women's active participation in politics. Not surprisingly, it was indeed during such a transitional period in the political histories of Sri Lanka, India, the Philippines, and Pakistan that women became the chief executives of these nations. The pattern of career development of the second generation of women legislators also suggests that major transitional periods of political power facilitate women's entry into national politics, even though the particulars of historical circumstances and the electoral system in which the second-generation women legislators find themselves are vastly different from those of the pioneer generation.

For example, all three second-generation elected legislators first contested at elections held in the transitional periods from one republic to another and, except for Kim Ok-son, won. Kim Ok-son first ran for a legislative seat in the transitional period from the First to the Second Republic but was unable to win as an independent. (See Chapter 6 for a discussion on the importance of the party affiliation for electoral successs. Kim Ok-son won in the seventh general elections, endorsed by a major opposition party.) Kim Yun-dok, who was endorsed by a major opposition party, won her first campaign in a National Assembly election that was held in the transitional period from the Third to the Fourth Republic. When Kim Chong-rye was first elected to the National Assembly as a ruling party candidate, the country was going through a transition from the Fourth to the Fifth Republic.

For these second-generation elected women legislators, personal experiences during the postliberation chaos (1945-48) and the tragic Korean War (1950-53), which raised their political consciousness and proved to be turning points in their lives, moved them to lifelong commitment to political careers. As to the appointed women legislators, it was the proportional party list system (which was adopted at the great transition from the Second Republic to the military-led Third Republic) that made their legislative careers possible. For most appointed women legislators, the invitation to join a government party provided a turning point for them to participate in national politics.

To sum up, the pattern of career developments of women politicians, from the three kingdoms era to modern Korea, suggests that Korean women's participation in national politics was made possible by a variety of special historical circumstances of the country that necessitated a radical departure from the traditional sexual division of labor.

NOTES

1. Oh (1982); H. Yi (1982).
2. Oh (1982:4). It is interesting to note that Indira Gandhi expressed the same opinion; see Dhawan (1985).
3. H. Yi (1982:251-52).
4. For details on the women candidates, see Lee and Kim (1976:123-24).
5. Lee and Kim (1976:126).
6. Son (1972:615).
7. For the roles students and the military played in Korean politics, see Oh (1975); Lovell (1975).
8. Oh (1975:123-24).
9. Lovell (1975:88).
10. C. Lee (1981).
11. Lovell (1975:189).

12. Lovell (1975:184-85) reports in detail on the youthfulness of the leadership since the military revolution in comparison with the previous two regimes.

13. The three women are not related despite their same surname. Kim is the most common surname in Korea and has many separate clans based on their places of origin. For interesting episodes concerning Korean values and attitudes regarding family names, see Kusano (1985:102-19).

14. It is noteworthy that both of the women cabinet ministers in Japan until the summer of 1989 were appointed by one man, Prime Minister Ikeda, in the early 1960s (see Robins-Mowry 1983:245).

15. Son (1972:252-64).

16. Son (1972:411-12).

17. According to Son (1972:413), Yim stated to Son during an interview that "it was the most rewarding period in my life. I was able to exert my best for Dr. Rhee, my eternal ideal, who to me was like a father, a husband, and an older brother."

18. Son (1972:439-41).

19. Ambassador Romulo of the Philippines, who was one of the important people who helped Yim Yong-sin in her diplomatic endeavors at the United Nations, remembered and praised her stubborn determination in his foreword to her biography, written by Son (1972).

20. For the details of both the domestic and international political situations during the winter of 1947-48, see Oliver (1978:119-50).

21. For the various views of the Korean situation held by the members of the U.N. Commission, see Oliver (1978:119-39); Son (1972:501-2).

22. For the process and implications of the establishment of the Rhee administration, see Ch'oe (1985).

23. Other women (e.g., Helen Kim, Pak Sung-ho, Hwang Sin-dok, and Pak Sun-ch'on) also actively participated in welcoming the United Nations Commission (Pak 1974-75:20).

24. Son (1972:503-4).

25. Son (1972:508).

26. Yim (1951:276).

27. Son (1972:543-44).

28. For more details, see KWA (1986:204-5).

29. McCune (1950:238).

30. KWA (1986:24).

31. Pak (1974-75:21).

32. Pak (1974-75:33).

33. The Minjudang should not be confused with the Han'guk Minjudang formed in September, 1945.

34. For an extensive survey of research on Korean political culture, see H. Kim (1983).

35. Yun (1979); Han (1984).

36. Oliver (1954).

37. *Maeil Sinbo,* October 18, 1945, as reported in National History Compilation Committee (NHCC) (1968:267).

38. KWA (1986:23-24).

39. *Chungang Ilbo* (U.S. edition), July 1 and 2, 1988.

40. Son (1972:626).

41. Scalapino (1981:142).

42. Cheon (1982).

43. Turner (1969:106).

44. Henderson (1968:101).

45. For experiences of women in the Third World, see Jayawardena (1986).

(*Above*) The Korean National
Assembly building. *Photograph by the author.*

(*Right*) Downtown Seoul,
where the juxtaposition of
traditional and Western archi-
tectural styles mirrors the
dual social structure.

(*Above*) Yim Yong-sin at the United Nations. *Courtesy of Yim Ch'ol-sun.*

(*Left*) Yim Yong-sin. *Courtesy of Kyonghyang Sinmun.*

(*Above*) Pak Sun-ch'on and her husband, Pyon Hi-yong. *Courtesy of
Yim Chung-bin.*

(*Right*) Pak Hyon-suk. *Courtesy of
Kyonghyang Sinmun.*

Kim Ch'ol-an, Pak Sun-ch'on, and Pak Hyon-suk during the fourth National Assembly (1958-60). *Courtesy of Yim Chung-bin.*

Kim Ch'ol-an at home in Kimch'on. *Photograph by the author.*

(*Right*) Representative Kim Ok-son. *Courtesy of* Kyonghyang Sinmun.

(*Below*) Representative Kim Ok-son greeting some of her constituents, members of a local Confucian club (1985). *Photograph by the author.*

(*Left*) Representative Kim Chong-rye. *Courtesy of Kim Chong-rye.*

(*Below*) Representative Kim Chong-rye visiting the home for the disabled in her constituency in Seoul. *Photograph by the author.*

Kim Yun-dok and her husband, Yu Hong-kun. *Courtesy of Kim Yun-dok.*

Representative Kim Hyon-ja reading from the Bible at the chapel in the National Assembly building during a monthly breakfast prayer meeting (1985). *Photograph by the author.*

6

Winning Legislative Seats

The fact that only seven women were able to win in the general elections during the four decades since the establishment of the Republic of Korea in 1948 bespeaks the tremendous difficulties women face in elective. politics. How then did the seven women manage to win? What were their success formulas?

ELECTORAL SUCCESS

Of the seven elected women legislators, four women won their elections at their first try, one at her second, and two at their third attempt. Six of the seven were reelected, while the remaining one served in the legislature again as an appointed member. Thus all seven women served in the National Assembly for at least two terms. They won sixteen seats in total during the thirteen National Assembly elections between 1948 and 1988 (see Table 1.1).

The professional dimensions of the life histories of elected women legislators suggest that the personal variables for election success of female candidates include (1) the possession of prestigious credentials to seek a legislative seat, (2) their organizational affiliations, and (3) the strength of regional roots.

Prestigious Credentials

"What has Yi Ki-bung done for his country? Did he ever participate in independence fighting?"[1] These rhetorical questions, which Yim Yong-sin posed in her criticism of her competitor for the vice-presidency in the March 1960 election, indicate the credential value of having been an independence fighter for a political aspirant of the prerevolution era. Indeed, the pioneer women legislators of the prerevolution era possessed the honorable credentials of having fought for national independence, which signified that they were the equals of their male colleagues. In addition, all the pioneer women legislators (except for Kim Ch'ol-an) had occupied high government offices prior to their legislative careers.

The cases of four women legislators who were elected at their first attempt suggest that the possession of prestigious credentials at the time of candidacy was of crucial importance for the successful election of women candidates. They had served as either a cabinet minister or an appointed legislator before their first candidacy. Through their service in the administration or legislative body, therefore, the four women (Yim Yong-sin, Pak Hyon-suk, Kim Yun-dok, and Kim Chong-rye) had acquired social prestige and political fame at the national level before they ran for a seat in the National Assembly for the first time and won.

For example, Yim Yong-sin, who became the first woman legislator of South Korea, not only possessed the credentials of having been an independence fighter but also had acquired national fame and respect for her diplomatic activities at the United Nations and was serving as minister of commerce and industry when she ran in the special election in Andong in 1949. Yim Yong-sin won the special election against several major male contenders—including Chang T'aek-sang, the first minister of foreign affairs. Judging by a sample of her campaign speeches, it was her remarkable political and diplomatic activities coupled with her forceful actions as minister of commerce and industry and the personal endorsement of President Rhee that proved to be unbeatable, even though her male opponents tried hard to criticize her on personal grounds.[2] She was fifty years old at the time.

Pak Sun-ch'on, however, was unable to win in the first general election even though she had also been an independence fighter and had been active in postliberation politics. President Rhee then appointed her to the powerful Board of Inspection. By the time Pak Sun-ch'on ran in the second National Assembly election, she had to her advantage not only campaign experience in the previous general election but also the prestigious credential of having served honorably as a high official. Her activities as a member of the powerful Board of Inspection had been well covered in the daily newspapers.[3]

When Pak Sun-ch'on ran again in the same Chongno-kap district in Seoul, her former campaign workers reassembled. Many women supporters sent gold rings and *kumbinyo* (ornamental solid gold rods which are used in married women's traditional coiffures) as their contributions to her campaign fund. Pak Sun-ch'on wrote that thanks to such enthusiastic support by women, she did not have to worry about money.

Experienced and more knowledgeable about the game of election campaigning, Pak Sun-ch'on and her campaigners worked hard with a sort of vengeful determination and comfortably won the race. Pak garnered 11,251 votes to her opponent's (Chang Hu-yong) 9,212.[4] She was fifty-three years old when she started her illustrious legislative career, which included serving in the legislature for five terms and assuming the leadership of a major opposition party after the military revolution of 1961.

Kim Ch'ol-an, who lacked the prestige of having served as a high official, failed to win a legislative seat in the first two general elections. However, she was able to achieve nationwide fame by her valiant actions during the Korean War (1950-53), which helped her to win with a huge majority of votes in the third general election held after the war in 1954. Since the Korean War proved to be an important turning point in her political career, let us here detail her wartime activities, which she related during the interview.

Kim Ch'ol-an accompanied the local chair of the women's organization to Seoul to attend a meeting in 1950 after the second general election was over. The war broke out while she was in Seoul on this trip. The bridge over the Han River was bombed soon after the North Korean invasion of Seoul, and people clambered into small boats to cross the river. Kim Ch'ol-an said that she spontaneously took charge of the scrambling crowd there, making them proceed in a more orderly fashion, letting others go ahead before she finally crossed the Han in the last boat. On her way home she came across a small stray group of hungry soldiers fleeing from Seoul. She fed them with potatoes gathered from the field and boiled over the fire she made by breaking up the wooden gates of an abandoned house. She also tended injured soldiers and rallied other women to help her.

Later on, in Taegu, as deputy director of the Korea Young Women's Corps (Taehan Yoja Ch'ongnyon-dan), Kim Ch'ol-an was asked by Cho Pyong-ok, minister of Home Affairs, to deliver roadside speeches to the citizens informing them of the war situation. At the request of President Rhee, Kim went to the front in Yongch'on dressed in military attire. When no government officials moved to relieve the starving refugees, Kim Ch'ol-an dared to break open a government grain store and assured the hungry crowd that she would take full responsibility for the action. She was also sent to P'yongyang to observe the war situation. There she enlisted the U.S. military to help the people of P'yongyang to cross the Taedong River. Upon her return she gave a report of her observation trip at the National Theater in Seoul. Her constituency greatly appreciated her courageous, dedicated service and expressed their disappointment with their National Assembly representative, who was nowhere to be seen.

Thus, in the spring of 1954 when Kim Ch'ol-an paid a house call to one of the village elders in Kumnung, the man rushed to the gate *poson pallo* (in his stocking feet) to welcome her.[5] He profusely complimented her for

her valorous actions and benevolent leadership during the war.   He
assured her of victory this time, advising her just to sit and wait for the
news without spending even a penny on an election campaign. This was
the man who responded with a perfunctory nod to her visits during the
two previous elections and deigned to say: "I suppose women may also
run."   To this hero's welcome, the happy political aspirant gave the
sheepish reply: "Well, I don't think I am running any more!" Kim Ch'ol-an
told me that she not only won the race but became one of the four
legislators who garnered an overwhelming majority of votes in the third
general election by winning 20,078 votes.[6] When she finally became a
lawmaker, she was forty-two years old.

When Pak Hyon-suk first ran in the fourth general election and won the
race, her political credentials included her active participation in the
independence movement and high-level government service as a member
of the Board of Inspection and as a minister without portfolio in the cabinet
of President Rhee. Therefore, although she initially faced sexual prejudice
against her candidacy, Pak Hyon-suk won the race backed by her superior
credentials and the endorsement of the Liberal Party. She was fifty-eight
years old when she became a lawmaker.

Kim Yun-dok had the prestige of having been an appointed legislator
before she first ran for a legislative seat in the ninth general election as a
candidate of the major opposition party and won. Kim Chong-rye had
been a member of the Legislative Council for National Safeguarding before
she ran in the 1981 election as a candidate of the Democratic Justice Party.

Having thus achieved nationwide fame and prestige prior to their
successful candidacies in the National Assembly elections, these women
legislators were able to win as distinguished female candidates who were
exceptionally qualified to seek a legislative career.

Organizational Affiliations

Compared with the first two terms of the National Assembly, when the
majority of the legislators had been independents, a drastic change in the
political climate took place in the third National Assembly: 114 out of the
203 members belonged to the Liberal Party, which had been created by
President Syngman Rhee three years prior to the 1954 election.

Yim Yong-sin and Pak Sun-ch'on, the two female members of the
second National Assembly, lost their seats in the third National Assembly
election in 1954, while Kim Ch'ol-an finally won after her unsuccessful
attempts in the two previous parliamentary elections.

It appeared that differences in organizational affiliation played a major
role in the surprising results. Kim Ch'ol-an was endorsed by the Liberal

Party. Yim Yong-sin stood as a candidate of the Korea Women's National Party, which she helped found after Liberation and headed as its president until it was disbanded after the military revolution. Pak Sun-ch'on, who had refused to join the Liberal Party (as described in Chapter 5), ran as an independent and lost the 1954 election. Pak Sun-ch'on was soon invited to participate in the creation of an opposition party. When the Democratic Party (Minjudang) was launched in September 1955, Pak Sun-ch'on became its advisor and vice-chair of the Central Committee.

Membership in a major political party has become a crucial factor for a successful political career since the third general election. Those candidates who are either independents or members of minor political parties now have very slim chances of winning an election.[7]

Moreover, from the 1958 general election onward, the right combination of ruling versus opposition party endorsement and rural versus urban constituency became a critical factor for a successful candidacy. The general perception was that the ruling party candidates had a better chance to win a race in the rural constituencies, and the opposition party candidates in the urban constituencies.[8]

The cases of the three women legislators elected to the fourth National Assembly in 1958 support this common perception. Both Kim Ch'ol-an and Pak Hyon-suk had been endorsed by the ruling Liberal Party in the rural constituencies of Kumnung and Kumhwa respectively. By contrast, Pak Sun-ch'on, who became a major figure in the opposition Democratic Party, was elected from a constituency in Pusan, the second largest city in Korea.

In the fifth general election, held after the student uprising, those who had been members of the Liberal Party were discredited across the board. Pak Sun-ch'on wrote that the enthusiastic mood of the people for the Democratic Party (DP) was such that almost anybody with a DP endorsement could win a legislative seat.[9] The fifth general election held in 1960 was thus an exception to the hypothesis discussed above concerning the advantageous combination of party affiliation and the location of constituency. The ruling Democratic Party, for example, won fifteen of the sixteen electorates in Seoul, where candidates of major opposition parties traditionally enjoy higher chances of winning the race.[10]

Pak Sun-ch'on, of course, won the race easily in Pusan as a member of the Democratic Party, but her two colleagues in the fourth National Assembly who were members of the Liberal Party failed to win their races. Pak Hyon-suk ran as an independent at the fifth general election but failed to be reelected to the legislature, largely due to her previous affiliation with the disgraced Liberal Party. The political career of Kim Ch'ol-an as a two-term assemblywoman was also nipped in the bud in the turbulent political climate after the student uprising. She tried to vindicate her legislative career and the Liberal Party by running as an independent candidate in the fifth National Assembly election and as a member of the Liberal Party in the sixth. She was not only unsuccessful both times but even imprisoned for alleged election fraud after the fifth National Assembly election.

A more recent example of party politics is Hyon Ki-sun, who was appointed to the short-lived tenth National Assembly as a member of the ruling Democratic Republican Party (DRP). Hyon Ki-sun ran unsuccessfully in the eleventh National Assembly election as a candidate of the People's Party (Kungmindang), formed mainly by former members of the defunct DRP. It was in a spirit of vindicating the former (Park) regime that Hyon rather valiantly plunged into politics. Although a daily newspaper reported her to be a strong candidate,[11] it was predictable that she would be unable to win the race as a female member of a minor party.

Hyon stated during the interview that her defeat was due to lack of funds as well as her naivete about party politics. As a female candidate of a minor party, she was unable to raise much funds for her campaign. Political funds, of course, play an important role in winning election. Candidates of the ruling party in general are believed to be in a more advantageous position for raising campaign funds over those belonging to opposition or minor parties.

In any case, the individual experiences of the three second-generation women legislators (Kim Ok-son, Kim Yun-dok, and Kim Chong-rye) who were elected after the military revolution seemed to underscore the importance of the endorsement of a major political party (be it the ruling or the major opposition party) in their successful political careers.

Kim Ok-son ran for a legislative seat as an independent in the fifth and sixth general elections without success. She confessed to me that she was running blindly in those elections, without realizing the power of the organizational affiliation for a successful candidacy. When she finally won a legislative seat in the seventh general election, Kim Ok-son had not only more experience in managing an effective campaign but also had the endorsement of the main opposition party (Sinmindang).

Kim Yun-dok is unique among the seven elected political women in that she followed the conventional route to becoming a legislator. Kim Yun-dok joined the Democratic Party in 1956 when she was twenty years old and had been married for three months. Kim Yun-dok was working as director of the Women's Bureau of her party when she was given the nomination for the appointed membership to the eighth National Assembly in 1971. Thus, she had been an active member of the major opposition party for fifteen years before she became an appointed legislator. She then contested in the 1973 general election for the ninth National Assembly with the endorsement of her party and won the race. She was reelected to the tenth National Assembly.

The sudden legislative career of Kim Chong-rye provides another dramatic example of the powerful effect of organizational affiliation. A political activist for more than thirty years, Kim Chong-rye had been known as a staunch opponent of the military rule and the Park regime throughout the 1960s and 1970s. However, her meeting with General Chun in May, 1980, brought about a turning point in her political career, as was discussed in Chapter 5. She joined the Democratic Justice Party (DJP) and was elected to the eleventh National Assembly as a member of the ruling DJP. Kim Chong-rye intimated during the interview that the organizational support she received from her party was crucial to her victory.

It is interesting to note how the women legislators in this study differ in their relationships with women's organizations. In general, the pioneer-generation political women had closer working relations with and strong support of the members of their own sex than did the majority of the second-generation women legislators (both elected and appointed), who have worked in predominantly male environments.

The difference is in part a reflection of the changes that have taken place in the nature of women's organizations. From the 1920s (after the March First Movement) until liberation, members of women's organizations were committed to the dual liberation: their country's liberation from Japanese occupation and women's liberation from patriarchal oppression.[12] And during the prerevolution era, women's organizations such as the Korea Women's Association and the Korea Women's National Party were directly involved in national politics.

Yim Yong-sin, for instance, headed the Korea Women's National Party (KWNP) for more than a decade until the military government disbanded all political parties. The KWNP made several proposals for egalitarian marital life, such as a marriage rule for monogamy, equal punishment for adultery, and separate property ownership for married couples.[13] During the Korean War, Yim Yong-sin organized the Women's Association for National Defense, and later headed the Korea Women's Association.

For Kim Ch'ol-an, her involvement in the local chapter of the Patriotic Women's Organization (Aeguk Puinhoe) served as "the glow of a firefly" leading her eventually into the political arena. Kim Ch'ol-an ran as a member of the Patriotic Women's Organization and the Korea Women's Association in the first and second general elections respectively.

Pak Sun-ch'on also worked among women as vice-president of the Women's League for Nation Building (Kon'guk Punyo Tongmaeng). The League declared the great task of "women's liberation" to be a major goal of their organization. Pak Sun-ch'on ran for the first three National Assembly elections as an independent, supported by women's organizations. As mentioned earlier, many enthusiastic women supporters sent their jewelry, such as gold rings and *kumbinyo*, to contribute to her campaign.[14]

When a new civil code was being drafted after the Korean War, several women's organizations combined their forces to submit a proposal for a family inheritance law. A Committee for Women's Rights Advocacy (Yokwon Ongho Wiwonhoe) was formed, and Pak Hyon-suk was nominated to the presidency.[15]

The Korean War, however, had a deep impact on all major social institutions and dampened women's enthusiastic activism for sexual equality.[16] By the end of the war, conservative attitudes and traditional values reemerged as a majority force. The military became a central institution, and national security and anticommunism justified the authoritarian rule of the Rhee regime. Women's participation in politics declined, and active female political participation was limited to a small number of women leaders in political parties and women's organizations.

During the latter part of the First Republic, the leaders of some women's organizations were involved in politics as blind supporters of the Liberal Party and the Rhee regime. They were vehemently opposed to Yim Yong-sin's candidacy challenging Yi Ki-bung of the Liberal Party for the vice-presidency. With the collapse of the First Republic, staff members of the Korea Women's Association and the Korea Young Women's Corps were sent to jail for their participation in election frauds.[17]

A phase of transition and backlash in women's activism set in after the military coup. In 1961, the military government disbanded all voluntary associations as well as political parties. Two years later, when women's organizations were allowed to reform, they opted to be politically neutral. During the decade of the 1960s, the activities of women's organizations were limited to those concerning self-improvement and volunteer social work for "national reconstruction." Women's liberation activities were not pursued.[18]

Therefore, in contrast to the pioneer-generation women legislators, who had worked as leaders of women's organizations, elected women legislators of the second generation (except Kim Chong-rye) had little to do with women's organizations. Neither Kim Ok-son nor Kim Yun-dok were actively involved in women's organizations, although the former was engaged in social work for women by providing a home for widows and orphans and building schools for girls.

It was only in the 1970s that people started to think of women's problems as legitimate social issues and the movement for Family Law revision was resumed. The U.N. Decade for Women contributed to the reawakening of women's consciousness. The Chun administration, for instance, created the Korea Women's Development Institute and ratified the U.N. Declaration of the Elimination of Discrimination against Women, with some modifications. Several women legislators appointed by President Chun were working as leaders of women's organizations (as is shown later in this chapter). But other appointed women legislators said that they did not belong to women's organizations, because working among men as equals was a more effective way to improve women's status than joining women's organizations.

Regional Roots

It was noted earlier that the urban constituency-cum-opposition party and rural constituency-cum-ruling party came to be regarded as the general formula for winning National Assembly elections. The assumption behind the theory is that since the ruling party is in a better financial position to support their candidates, the ruling party candidates often win votes by offering their electors various material gifts, and that it is easier to influence the rural voters in this fashion. It is believed that better-educated urban voters tend to be more critical of the ruling party than rural electors, who tend to cast their votes in exchange for personal favors received from their candidates.

However, the combinations of party affiliation and electoral district of the women legislators of the postrevolution era were the complete opposites of the generally accepted formula for election success. Kim Ok-son and Kim Yun-dok, both of whom belonged to the opposition party, were given rural districts. Kim Chong-rye, as a member of the ruling party, confronted an urban constituency in Seoul. Their cases suggest that even though there is no legal requirement for the residency of the candidates in their constituencies, the regional roots of the candidates in their constituencies is an important ingredient for success and can be powerful enough to overcome an adverse combination of constituency and party affiliation.

Kim Ok-son was a native of Ch'ungch'ong province. By the time she won election as an opposition party candidate in a rural district of Ch'ungch'ong, she had worked hard for more than a decade to improve the social welfare and education of the people of Ch'ungch'ong by building schools, churches, and a home for war-stricken widows and orphans. To many of her constituents, Kim Ok-son was seen as a benevolent leader working singlemindedly for the welfare of the people of her hometown region. The members of her clan and those people who benefited from her work (such as widows, orphans, students, and members of her churches) expressed their appreciation by campaigning vigorously to bring her victory. Her first two candidacies as an independent were unsuccessful, largely due to her lack of experience in politics. By the time she ran for the third time in 1967, however, Kim Ok-son had acquired firm local support, the endorsement of a major political party, and sufficient political savvy to wage a year-long legal battle to claim her victory over the election rigging of her rival candidate from the ruling party.

Kim Yun-dok, as a native of Cholla province, had the advantage of running in a constituency in Cholla province (Naju and Kwangsan) that included her husband's hometown. However, the combination of her opposition-party affiliation and a rural constituency was regarded as an obstacle to winning the race. Kim Yun-dok's blunt statements, "Pak Sun-ch'on and Yim Yong-sin did it with ease" and "my political career as a female member of the opposition party was the way of the Cross," may be understood as testimony to the tremendous difficulties a woman without a presidential connection has to face to pursue a political career in the opposition camp, especially in the postrevolution era.

Kim Yun-dok said that she won the election by working with her husband as a team; she campaigned mainly in the public, formal arena, while her businessman husband rounded up the support of his friends and relatives and met with male voters in public, informal settings, often entertaining them with drinks (see Chapter 7 for a further discussion of contrastive behavioral patterns in the public/private spheres and formal/informal situations).

Kim Chong-rye said that her constituency, Songbuk-ku, is one of the poorest wards in Seoul and that a large number of its residents came from Cholla province. It is quite apparent, then, that the fact that Kim Chong-rye came from a poor family in Cholla favorably influenced the decision makers of her party to endorse her as their candidate in Songbuk-ku. The rationale behind the party decision, of course, was that, despite a disadvantageous combination of urban constituency-cum-ruling party, the regional roots of Kim Chong-rye would play a positive role in winning the support of the many low-income working families of Cholla origin residing in Songbuk-ku, given the heavy regionalism that still prevails in Korea.[19]

ELECTORAL SYSTEM

There was not one elected woman legislator in the thirteenth National Assembly. Fourteen women ran in the regional consitutencies in the thirteenth general election in 1988, but all failed to win. In contrast, two of seven women candidates in the twelfth general election were successful at the polls in 1985. A comparative analysis of the contrasting outcomes between the 1985 and 1988 elections suggests the significance of the electoral system in affecting women's chances of winning the election.

In the 1985 general election, the electoral system was based on multiple-member constituencies in which two of the candidates were elected. The two women who won the elections in 1985, Kim Chong-rye and Kim Ok-son, captured the second largest votes in their constituencies. In the 1988 general election, the electoral system was changed to single-member constituencies, and both Kim Chong-rye and Kim Ok-son lost their elections. Among the fourteen unsuccessful women candidates for the 1988 general election, four (including Kim Chong-rye) garnered the second highest number of votes in their electoral districts.[20] This suggests that some women candidates could very well have won in the 1988 election had the electoral system continued to be based on multiple-member constituencies, as in the previous elections.

A brief cross-national comparison of the varying degree of women's legislative participation below demonstrates that the type of electoral system is a crucial factor in affecting female representation in national legislative bodies. Although the rates of women's representation in New Zealand and Canada have risen considerably over the last few years with single-member plurality voting systems,[21] the experiences of women in Europe, Asia, and the United States clearly indicate that proportional representation party list systems are conducive to higher female representation.

For instance, in Scandinavia, the percentage of women members in national legislatures ranged between 24 percent in Denmark and 35 percent in Norway in 1985.[22] A recent cross-national report on women legislators found that Sweden had the highest ratio of women (38 percent) in the national legislative bodies in 1988.[23] What is noteworthy about the electoral systems of Scandinavian countries is that the recruitment of their legislators is based on proportional representation party list systems, which contribute to high female representation. In the case of West Germany, where half the Bundestag is elected by a single-member constituency system and half by a proportional representation party list system, the great majority of women became legislators via the lists.[24]

In contrast, in the United Kingdom and the United States, whose electoral systems are based on single-member constituencies, the percentage of women members in the House of Commons of the United Kingdom was 4.3 percent in 1987, while women members made up 5.0 percent in the House of Representatives of the United States in 1986.[25]

In Asia, the "reserved seats" election system of the Republic of China guarantees women approximately 10 percent of the seats on its legislative bodies, and women usually win more than their reserved allotment.[26] After the 1989 election for the upper house of the Diet, Japanese women occupied 13 percent of the chamber's seats, while female represenatation accounted for less than 2 percent in the more powerful lower house of the Diet.[27] The considerable difference in the ratio of female representation between the two houses of the Diet is rooted in part in the proportional representation party list system, which is utilized for the recruitment of the members of the upper house, but not for the lower house of the Diet. In Korea, six women who became legislators due to the proportional representation party list system made up 2 percent of the members of the National Assembly in 1989. Had the membership in the National Assembly been based exclusively on the election results of single-member constituencies, the Korean legislature could have become a veritable male bastion.

LEGISLATIVE APPOINTMENTS

While various episodes in the career development of elected women legislators intimate extraordinary difficulties for women candidates to win legislative seats, the patterns of career development of appointed women legislators indicate that for most of them their journey to the National Assembly was rather facile.

Since appointed legislators are supposed to represent diverse sectors of society, they come from a variety of occupational backgrounds, including women's organizations, political parties, academia, public administration, and mass media. Most of them were well-known leaders in their professional fields.

As to the recruitment of appointed legislators, there exist no clear-cut criteria. Moreover, the ruling and opposition parties apparently differ in their recruitment strategies, which are reflected in the predominance of appointed women legislators belonging to ruling parties. Opposition parties have appointed only four women to the National Assembly for the last two and a half decades: Pak Sun-ch'on to the seventh, Kim Yun-dok to the eighth, Hwang San-song to the eleventh, and Pak Yong-suk to the thirteenth National Assembly. Prior to their appointments, three of the four held leadership positions within their parties while the remaining one was a well-known lawyer with political ambition. She joined the party just before her legislative appointment.

For the ruling party, which does not have to worry about its financial status, balanced representation in terms of professional backgrounds is regarded as an important consideration in its recruitment of appointed legislators. In the case of male appointed legislators, who are more numerous than their female counterparts, their regional backgrounds also counted as an important factor in their recruitment.

Since the Park regime, the leadership of the ruling party has often been accused of favoring people from Kyongsang province over those from Cholla province. Thus, when a former ambassador from Cholla was appointed to the National Assembly by President Chun, another former ambassador commented that the Cholla origin of his former colleague was a decisive factor for his selection from among several candidates who were retired ambassadors.

For opposition parties, however, the proportional representation party list system has become a major source of political funds. Political aspirants can secure seats in the National Assembly by paying huge sums of money as part of their contributions to the party.

For example, a male informant who was a member of a major opposition party told me that he could have become an appointed member of the twelfth National Assembly by paying one hundred million *won* (over $112,000),[28] which would have placed him in the national constituency list as the thirteenth candidate. At the time, one of his friends among the party leaders predicted that fewer than ten appointive seats would be available and advised him to wait for the next term. However, the election resulted in a greater number of elected legislators from the opposition party than anticipated. Consequently, to the chagrin of my informant, seventeen men from his party found their way into the legislature as appointed members.

Kim Yun-dok said that she was approached before the twelfth general election by members of an opposition party who suggested she donate a large sum of money to the party in order to resume her legislative career. She said that she refused the offer because as a three-term legislator she felt insulted by such an offer and that what she wanted was an offer of a constituency instead.

In general, it is believed that monetary donations are not involved in the case of appointed legislators from ruling parties. An appointed woman legislator from a ruling party declared that she and her colleagues did not spend a penny in order to become appointive members of the National Assembly.

Appointed assemblywomen may be divided into four subcategories on the basis of the extent of political socialization prior to their entry into the legislature: (1) those who held higher degrees in the subjects of political science or law but had no experience in the political arena (who may be referred to as political "savants"); (2) those who gained a high level of political socialization by working for the government or a political party (who may be referred to as political "administrators"); (3) those whose occupation brought them into close contact with politicians and government officials (who may be referred to as political "observers"); and (4) those who lacked political socialization (who may be referred to as political "novices").

It should be noted, however, that the categories of appointed women legislators described above are not mutually exclusive; for some women they overlap. Among the administrators were women who had studied law and gained political experience by joining a political party voluntarily. Kim Yun-dok, for example, majored in law, worked for an opposition party, and then was appointed to the legislature before she became an elective member of the National Assembly.

Many of the savants had Ph.D. degrees and were teaching at universities before their recruitment. The administrators had either directed the Women's Bureau within a party or had worked as government officials. The observer category is composed mainly of newspaper reporters who had covered government and sociopolitical activities. Those classified as novices worked either as women's organization leaders or held leadership positions in professional associations or civic groups. Immediately preceding their entries into the legislature, 36 percent (eight) of the twenty-two informants belonged to the savant category, 18 percent (four) to the administrator, 23 percent (five) to the observer, and another 23 percent (five) to the novice category.

The recountals of the process of legislative recruitment showed a distinct pattern among the four categories of appointed women legislators of differing motivations and attitudes about their participation in national politics. The administrators were active seekers of political office while most women in the novice, observer, and savant categories were passive appointees, who denied political ambitions on their part and emphasized the arbitrary, obligatory aspects of the recruitment process, which suggests that their legislative appointments were offers they were unable to refuse.

A "novice" informant said that her appointment was "quite unexpected and a great surprise." Another novice stated, "When they urged me to join the party [DRP], I found myself shuddering." A third novice said:

The recruitment came "out of the blue" [informant's own phrase in English]. My husband then was out of the country on a business trip, and I was unable to wait for his return to discuss the matter with him. After I accepted the offer and signed my name to join the party, I came home, went to my room, locked the door, and cried.

An "observer" informant said:

In my polite refusal, I tried to maintain a sense of humor and pointed out to the two agents that even my English was too poor for them to consider me as a worthy candidate.[29] They then showed me the list in the president's own handwriting, saying that it must be sent to the printers before midnight.

A "savant" stated:

It was not a matter of choice. It is just like I did not choose my sex. I was pushed. Nobody really believes me.

These negative responses of women legislators to their recruitments make better sense when one considers the cultural and political context of contemporary Korea. They reflect not only the general perception that politics is men's work but also the particularly volatile political climate of the nation.

From the First to the Fifth Republic, for instance, the transfer of power was accomplished by violent means, such as student uprisings, military coups, and assassination. Discontinuities in the political system were accompanied by emotional reactions against their predecessors; those officials and politicians who served under previous regimes were instantly discredited, often indicted on corruption charges, and/or banned for varying periods of time from seeking public office. One of the "novice" women quoted above thought that a major reason for her appointment was due to her professional history, which had been "unsullied" by active involvement in politics under the previous regimes. Under these precarious circumstances, many people want to avoid strong identification with any particular political party or regime, while some tend to actively take advantage of their powerful positions during their tenure in high government office.

Another important factor accounting for negative responses was that academic women might have to sacrifice their tenured positions at universities in order to serve in the legislature, which is normally a one-term appointment. Ewha Women's University, for example, disallows political involvement of its faculty members. Kim Ok-kil, former president of Ewha, advocated a sense of professional mission and stated that that was why she made it her policy not to rehire those professors who had left Ewha for nonacademic occupations.[30] One "savant" informant had to resign from her post as dean of the College of Law at Ewha upon her appointment to the ninth National Assembly. After her legislative career, she spent almost three years at home before she resumed her academic career at Songsin Women's University, where her former legislative colleague, Yi Suk-chong, was president. Another savant quoted above stated that her appointment meant risking her career in academia.

In addition, anticipation of role strain in their family lives prevented married females from agreeing to their recruitment. The first "novice" informant quoted above stated that when her husband returned home from his trip abroad, he was shocked to hear the news of her appointment to the legislature and would not talk to her for several days. Another novice said that her first response to the recruiting agents was, "Let me consult my husband," but the agents insisted that it had nothing to do with her husband and that she had to make her own decision right then and there.

A savant informant with a Ph.D. in political science told me that she experienced ambivalent feelings at her recruitment into the legislature. She felt honored and welcomed the opportunity to practice the theories she had learned and taught. However, it was her husband, also a Ph.D. in political science, who had the ambition to become a politician. Thus her siblings, as well as her young children, reacted to her legislative appointment by saying that they would have preferred to have her husband become a legislator before she did. For several days after the announcement of her appointment, she said she had her phone disconnected whenever her husband was home, so that the congratulatory phone calls might not irritate him. Throughout her tenure, she had to be extremely careful not to hurt her husband's feelings. (After she completed her tenure, her husband also became a lawmaker and served in the legislature for two terms.)

By contrast, positive responses came mostly from the administrators, to whom appointments meant achieving the pinnacles of their political careers. They were satisfied to be accorded recognition for their abilities and for their contributions to the party, which their appointments signified. An "administrator" informant, who has a supportive husband and had been involved both in business and party politics before her legislative appointment, declared that she was the proudest among her colleagues due to the "proper processes" involved in her becoming a legislator. She hoped that her party leadership would recognize her as a truly committed politician and give her a chance to prove it. She was reappointed to the thirteenth National Assembly.

Some "observers" also frankly admitted their pleasure in being honored by appointments to the legislative body. A former journalist and writer, who had relished her new position as an appointed legislator, was pleased to be appointed to another high office at the end of her active one-term tenure in the National Assembly.

Some of the positive respondents did not hesitate to criticize the negative respondents for emphasizing the compulsory elements of the recruitment processes in the ruling camp. They argued that if one truly did not want the job, one could always find a way to refuse the offer. As an example, they spoke of a professor at Ewha who adamantly refused the offer of a legislative seat in the twelfth National Assembly, threatening to emigrate if they insisted. They also stated that there were many women who eagerly sought appointive memberships to the National Assembly. In fact, one negative effect of the legislative appointment practice is that many female political aspirants prefer to become legislators by appointment rather than going through the electoral process to build their own political basis and enhance their stature as legitimate politicians. One appointed woman legislator from an opposition party, for example, stated that her party at first urged her to run in a regional constituency in Seoul, but she decided against such a suggestion because she did not think she would win the race through the elctoral process.

For comparison, I applied the categories devised for appointed women legislators to the male appointed lawmakers of the Democratic Justice Party in the twelfth National Assembly. There were 276 members in the twelfth National Assembly, 92 (one-third) of whom were appointed members.[31] Of the 92, 61 belonged to the the ruling Democratic Justice Party (DJP). The remaining 31 appointed members belonged to opposition parties and included no women. The sex composition of the appointed members of the DJP was 6 female and 55 male originally, but because of the resignation of a female member (Pak Hye-kyong), it became 5 female and 56 male. Due to the lack of data on the new male member who replaced Pak, the male sample consisted of 55 initial members.

Among the 55, there were 6 "savants" (11 percent), 27 "administrators" (49 percent), 17 "observers" (31 percent), and 5 "novices" (9 percent) (who were former military men with no other occupational experiences in private or public sectors of society). The average age of the male sample was 48; the youngest was 42 and the oldest 70. The average age of their 5 female counterparts was 52; the youngest was 45 and the oldest 56. The median age of women legislators of this study at the start of their legislative careers was 49; the youngest was 34 and the oldest 60.

The comparison revealed the predominance of administrators in the male sample as the most noticeable difference in background characteristics of the female and male samples. In fact, a most striking difference between the male and female appointed legislators was their occupational backgrounds in civil service. Of the male members, 35 percent (nineteen of the fifty-five) were former government officials. In comparison, none of the five female members in the twelfth National Assembly served in the government before their appointments.

Another significant aspect of their professional careers was that 38 percent (twenty-one) of the male appointed lawmakers had already served in the legislature prior to their appointments to the twelfth National Assembly. In comparison, only one of their five female counterparts (20 percent) had the experience of serving in the legislature before her reappointment in 1985. However, three of the six (50 percent) women legislators of the thirteenth National Assembly had served in the legislature during the Fifth Republic. This new phenomenon is significant evidence of the continuity in the political elite from the Fifth to the Sixth Republic, whose transition of power was achieved peacefully for the first time in the history of the Republic of Korea after massive demonstrations in June 1987.

NOTES

1. Son (1972:604).
2. Son (1972:555-58).
3. Her activities as a member of the Board of Inspection included voting for a resolution that called for the dismissal of the Minister of Commerce and Industry, Yim Yong-sin, over the "Choson Leather Incident" (Pak 1974-75:22). Yim Yong-sin resigned in June, 1949. The matter was brought to the court, which declared Yim Yong-sin not guilty in September, 1949 (Son 1972:567).
4. Pak (1974-75:23).
5. The phrase *poson pallo* signifies being in a great hurry.
6. For more deails, see Lee and Kim (1976:124-26).
7. For instance, there were only two independents (Yang Chong-kyu from Cheju-do and Yi Yong-taek from North Kyongsang province) among the 276 members of the twelfth National Assembly (NA 1985).
8. For an analysis of the hypothesis, see Yun (1979:451-73).
9. Pak (1974-75:40).
10. Yun (1979:472).
11. *Dong-a Ilbo*, February 25, 1981.
12. For a detailed discussion of the women's movement in the 1920s, see Y. Kim (1979:259-66).
13. H. Lee (1985); PCC (1959:238-55).
14. Pak (1974-75:23).
15. H. Lee (1985:326).
16. For an extensive discussion on the effects of the Korean War on the society as a whole, see H. Lee (1985).
17. KWA (1986:32-33).
18. H. Lee (1985:319).
19. For a brief description of regionalism in Korea, see De Vos and Lee (1981:162-63).
20. Central Commission for Election Management (CCEM) (n.d.).
21. Randall (1987:141).
22. Randall (1987:103).
23. *Han'guk Ilbo* (Hawaii edition), August 30, 1989.
24. Vallance (1979:151-52).
25. Randall (1987:101-2).
26. Chou and Clark (1986).
27. Smolowe (1989:25).
28. One U.S. dollar was equivalent to about 887 *won* in 1985.
29. For the implications of her statement, see Chapter 3, on education.
30. *Chungang Ilbo*, September 22, 1983.
31. NA (1985).

7

Patterns of Adaptive Response

Since the traits of a woman and a politician are generally perceived to be antithetical, a woman politician must confront the question of how to be an effective lawmaker after she wins an election.[1] For the women legislators of this study, the persistence of the hierarchical Confucian ideas about the proper roles and places for men and women further complicates their political life. "As a woman, I found it more difficult to figure out how to behave after my victory at the polls than before," said Kim Ch'ol-an.

How then have women legislators of this study responded to the tension generated by dual gender-role ideologies (one based on democratic principles of egalitarianism and the other on patriarchal attitudes of male superiority)?   What strategies have they adopted for their political efficacy?

PERSONAL STRATEGIES

A significant factor that directly affects the professional life of women legislators is that the process of decision making in Korean political culture is from the top down, and that personal factors rather than the intrinsic merits of an issue or policy often influence decisions.[2]   Hence, interpersonal relations with the top decision maker in the informal arena play an important part in professional effectiveness in formal political settings.

A by-product of the hierarchical, personal approach to decision-making processes is that everybody tries to seek direct contact with the top decision maker. One assemblywoman said that her constituents insist on seeing her personally for all kinds of minor problems rather than talk to her secretary or other assistants. If they are unable to meet with their representative personally, their next choice falls on a member of the immediate family of the representative, preferably the spouse of the lawmaker.

When members of her constituency came to Seoul to seek various kinds of assistance from their legislator Kim Yun-dok, for example, her husband often met them and took care of their accommodations and entertainment. He seemed to have regarded his wife's political career as a joint venture. When recollecting the stories of their past, he used the term "we" (*uri*) instead of "I" or "she."

The pattern of informal, personal approaches to decision making and problem solving especially burdens women legislators in their professional life because it means they themselves would have to approach their male colleagues in an informal, personal manner to build rapport, gather information, and be included in the political processes. Some women legislators try to solve the problem of isolation by developing close dyadic ties with male colleagues. Others make cordial individual contact with persons in power in informal settings, such as tea or lunch in a restaurant. Many seemed simply to follow the party line.

Yim Yong-sin wrote that she was unable to join her male colleagues when she found them gathered in little groups in the chambers of the National Assembly discussing something about "Acheson" in worried tones on January 13, 1950, "because women in Korea do not easily move into a circle of men."[3] After overhearing fragments of their grave conversations about Americans, dangers, armies, invasions, and so on, she rushed out of the Assembly to the office of her longtime friend, Vice-Chairman Yun Ch'i-yong. From him, Yim Yong-sin learned about the important speech Secretary Acheson had made on the previous day regarding the U.S. defense policy.

One appointed woman legislator in the twelfth National Assembly also acknowledged the problem of gaining timely access to information because of the barriers of the informal networking among the male politicians. She said that she tried to combat the problem by having private meetings over lunch with top government officials in the field of her legislative committee.

Another strategy that women legislators adopt to improve their political efficacy is to enlist the help of significant males. Husbands, sons, and male relatives can help assemblywomen by accompanying them to male-dominated gatherings and interacting with other men (politicians or voters) on behalf of their female kin, as did the husbands of Kim Ch'ol-an and Kim Yun-dok. Pak Sun-ch'on had her third son (Pyon Chun-ho) work as her secretary for a long time.[4]

Employing men rather than women as their personal assistants or secretaries seemed to offer a practical advantage for women legislators, since their male aides could more easily gather political information through informal contacts with their counterparts among male politicians.

For some women lawmakers who graduated from coed colleges, close *sonbae/hubae* (senior/junior) relationships with male alumni seemed another personal resource for their political efficacy.

Among women legislators of the twelfth National Assembly, Kim Ok-son had only men as her aide and secretaries. As an unmarried assemblywoman, she used to have her nephew work as her chief aide. Kim Chong-rye had both a female aide and a male secretary. In contrast, the majority of appointed women legislators had women as their personal aides and secretaries. Two of them, both of whom were former professors, stated that they felt an obligation to bring more women into political life and that was why they decided to employ women as their aides. However, one of them acknowledged that had it not been for her sense of obligation, there was no question that she would have chosen an experienced male aide, who would have been of more practical help to her personally. A third appointed woman legislator who used to work for a large women's organization stated that since most of the visitors to her office were women, she thought having a female aide would be more appropriate in her case.

What is interesting to note in this regard is that the two women legislators who were reappointed from the twelfth to the thirteenth National Assembly had men as their aides when I interviewed them. (In fact, both of these reappointed women legislators had been actively involved in political life before their initial entry into the National Assembly.) One of the two said that she chose a male aide because she thought a man would do a better job in dealing with the many male members of the National Pharmacologist Association, whose interest she had to represent as its vice-president. The other stated that her office was not an employment agency for women and that her selection of an aide was based on the ability of the individual to assist her well. She also indicated that a male aide was able to prevent the informational isolation of a woman legislator from her male colleagues by his close social interactions with the staff members of male legislators.

Other former women legislators who had male aides also pointed out various personal advantages of hiring men as their aides. One of them said that she had a female aide for the first two years but changed to a male aide after that. According to her experience, the mind of her female aide was always lingering on her home and only her body was in the office. Others also indicated that female aides lacked in their sense of responsibility and that they did not seem physically strong enough to withstand the pressures of the workplace. When the legislative session went on past midnight, for instance, female aides would not stay in the office until the session ended. In contrast, male aides not only stayed until the end of the session but also would report to the residence of their bosses early in the morning with briefings on the latest news. Thus, one may expect that women lawmakers who are personally ambitious about their political careers would hire men as their legislative aides.

Among the male legislators of the twelfth National Assembly, I found one man who had a female aide. She was a young woman with a law degree from the Seoul National University, who had received practical training in legislative affairs as a student intern. The male legislator, according to her, chose a woman as his aide because he loathed the cockiness of male aides. Moreover, he saved himself some money by offering her a lower salary than he would have paid a male aide of her qualifications! She said she felt a heavy responsibility as the first female aide to a male legislator, but at the same time was very frustrated in her position as his legislative aide because of the conflict of some fundamental values between her and her boss. She said that she was planning to go abroad for further study.

③ A third strategy for women legislators to improve their professional efficacy is to join male colleagues in their informal activities. One appointed woman legislator, unmarried and in her late forties at the time of appointment, said she took up golf after she became a legislator as a means of socializing with male colleagues. The strategy, however, has a hidden cost, because some conservative males would criticize their female colleagues behind their backs for their immodest "unwomanly" behaviors displayed in the informal social settings. A case in point is an appointed woman legislator who reportedly did not hesitate to drink in the company of her male colleagues. Single, in her late thirties, she had a Ph.D. in political science from a U.S. university and, unlike other women legislators, practiced sexual equality in her interactions with male colleagues, who apparently felt offended by her liberal behavior and spoke ill of her behind her back.

The assemblywoman who told me the above story was married and in her fifties and took pains not to express her own opinion on the matter, but there were subtle indications that she herself would never do such a thing. As an indirect comment on the above-mentioned assemblywoman whose unconventional behavior was criticized by male colleagues, my informant told me that when an assemblywoman joins her male colleagues to dine out, she is expected to leave discreetly sometime after the dinner, so that men could entertain themselves freely without the inhibiting presence of their female colleagues. If she does not do so, she will be criticized for being "a woman without *nunch'i*" (savoir faire or tact). One informant said that some men would half-jokingly suggest the departure time for their married female colleague by reminding her of her duty to look after her husband, "the big baby," at home.

In fact, having good *nunch'i* is essential to successful social life in Korean culture. Having good *nunch'i* means one is quick to adapt to the changes in situational factors. The behavioral patterns of people with good *nunch'i* indicate that they handle the contradictions of dual gender role ideologies by polarizing social arenas into public versus private spheres and into formal versus informal situations within each sphere of social action. This permits the rules that guide their social behavior to alternate in different social settings in accordance with the involved individuals' sex, age, and degree of familiarity.

Behavioral consequences of the alternating strategy are contrastive, gender-based patterns of social behavior that befit different spheres (public/private) and situations (formal/informal). The traditional Confucian gender-role ideology tends to guide people's behavior at group levels in public informal situations as well as in private formal situations. Democratic egalitarianism is more readily practiced either at the societal level in public and formal situations or at the individual level in private informal relationships (see Table 7.1).

A typical instance of private formal situations, where one is expected to follow the traditional gender-role ideology, is ancestor worship rites or funeral processions in which only men participate, while women play the role of helpers to men in making preparations for the rituals. In rural areas, for example, only men march in funeral processions as they travel from the village to the grave site. A few women take another route to the grave site to feed the participants.[5]

I observed how an elected woman legislator handled a private formal situation at her house (which was in the traditional Korean style), where she held a luncheon meeting for the local chapter committee of her party in late December. As soon as she arrived at home, she started to play the role of a hostess, supervising the kitchen staff and helping her aide to arrange the table. The men were served in the guest room first before women were served in the inner room next to the kitchen. The assemblywoman joined the women's table, which included a female vice-chair of the local chapter committee, her aide, and myself. After the main course of the meal was over, women joined men over tea and dessert. There the assemblywoman gave a little speech exhorting the committee members to complete their fund-raising efforts within December since it would be awkward to talk of money at the start of a new year. She then handed out to each committee member an envelope of money and a small gift for the new year to express her appreciation for their work for the last twelve months.

"Appropriate" gender-role behaviors for women professionals in public but informal situations require their prudent situational judgment based on good *nunch'i* (savoir faire or tact). An appointed woman legislator who is very much a political woman said that if her male colleagues suggested an

Table 7.1
Alternating Ideologies in Shifting Social Situations

	Behavioral Context		Prevalent Gender-Role Ideology		Level of of Interaction
P					
U	Formal		**Democratic Ideology**		Societal
B					
L					
I					
C	Informal		**Confucian Ideology**		Group
P					
R	Formal		**Confucian Ideology**		Group
I					
V					
A					
T	Informal		**Democratic Ideology**		Individual
E					

informal gathering, she would first try to find out whether it was to be held at an "eating place" or a "drinking place." Sometimes she would pose her male colleagues a direct question, such as "How many of you want me to join you?" in a good-humored way and join them after confirming their unanimous consent.

Kim Yun-dok said that she had never dined out with a male colleague before she became a legislator. During the early years of her political party life Kim Yun-dok encountered two kinds of reaction to her participation in political life from her male colleagues: those who sincerely cared for her advised her to return to domestic life, while others tried to use her sexually. She reminisced about the advice she received from a female police chief whose husband was a politician.[6] The woman told Kim Yun-dok to regard men as human beings only above their waists and as thieves and animals below their waists. As a young married woman launching a public life, Kim Yun-dok found this piece of advice very useful.

It was to her benefit to be sensitized to the importance of proper demeanor in interactions with the opposite sex in order to safeguard her political career, for the traditional double standard of sexual behavior continues to operate. A scandal or even a mere rumor of a sexual nature can be a fatal blow to a female public figure (especially if she is a married woman), while customarily it does not result in such a deadly consequence for a male public figure. This may explain why Kim Yun-dok never participated in informal evening gatherings with her male colleagues before she became a legislator.

When a professional woman dines out with her male colleagues even at their invitation, however, she is expected to exercise *nunch'i* and leave them sometime after the dinner so that they may freely entertain themselves without losing face. Kim Ok-son, for example, said that she usually stayed for about an hour at evening gatherings with her male colleagues.

By comparison, a female professional can interact with her male colleagues on an equal footing in public formal situations such as a business conference. Indeed, it is age and rank rather than sex that govern the rules of behavior in public formal relations. For instance, when one informant (who is in her late fifties and an administrator of a large women's organization) and a former general (who was more than ten years younger) had to meet each other for the first time to discuss a matter of mutual concern, the man, as her junior, felt it proper for him to first pay a courtesy call to her office.

Today, many men and women (especially of the younger generation) have peer relations in the private informal situations of friendship, courtship, and marital lives. The innovative use of the word *chagi* (self) as a term of address among young couples symbolically indicates among other things a move toward egalitarian male-female relationships in informal private situations. The Korean language, with its elaborate levels of honorifics, is a powerful conservative force in perpetuating the status quo of the patriarchal social order in which sex and age are major determinants of social status. Thus, the use of *chagi* as a term of address between couples, a use frowned upon by the older generation in general, is an important linguistic indicator of change toward a more egalitarian model in gender roles and male-female relationships, especially in private and informal situations.

More subtle but nevertheless powerful personal strategies to deal with the dual gender-role ideologies include the manipulation of symbols and cultural markers of gender, such as the style and color of clothes and hair, makeup, and speech behavior. Style of clothes seemed especially critical in creating the kinds of images women politicians wanted to convey to the public.

In Korean society, clothes have been an important instrument with which to make a symbolic statement about one's social status and identity. The inordinate degree of attention Korean people pay to their appearances has historical roots in the customs of the Yi dynasty.[7] As an estate society, it stipulated specific rules concerning the materials, colors, and styles of clothes for different social strata. Thus, one's physical appearance was a visual representation of one's social identity.[8]

The majority of elected women lawmakers chose to wear *hanbok* (the traditional Korean dress) in public life while appointed assemblywomen wore Western clothes. The dress styles of women legislators seemed to indicate their keen sensitivity to the importance of clothes in creating and maintaining proper images of themselves. It seemed that some assemblywomen, especially elected ones, wished to present themselves as virtuous conservative women in spite of the "masculine" occupation of their choice by wearing *hanbok*.

Among the pioneer-generation political women, Pak Sun-ch'on and Pak Hyon-suk chose to wear the traditional clothes. Pictures of Pak Sun-ch'on suggest that she wore only dark, solid colors except during the summer, while Pak Hyon-suk, according to her granddaughter, liked to wear beautiful, light-colored *hanbok*. Neither of them was seen in public wearing pants.

In contrast, Yim Yong-sin, who had lived in the United States for more than a decade, appeared to have worn Western pants as well as dresses most of the time and traditional costumes on special occasions. For example, in a 1946 picture of women marching down a street in Seoul to demonstrate against trusteeship, Yim Yong-sin stood out in the first row of the crowd as the only woman wearing a pair of pants and dark glasses. The pictures in her biography suggested that she normally wore Western-style clothes. A picture taken during her first election campaign in Andong, however, showed her wearing a traditional costume. Perhaps the fact that Andong, a *yangban* town, was one of the most conservative places in the country affected her decision to wear traditional clothes. The portrait hanging in the library building of Chungang University depicts Yim Yong-sin in *hanbok*, and the staff member who procured various life history materials of Yim Yong-sin for me referred to her as *halmoni* (grandmother). A grand matriarch seated in a dignified manner in *hanbok* may have been how Yim Yong-sin wanted the students and staff members of her Chungang University to remember her.

Kim Ch'ol-an said that when she was defeated, she felt relaxed enough to think of the next election strategy. However, when it became apparent that she won, she suddenly felt panicky, especially because she was to be *hongilchom* (literally, one red dot, meaning the only woman) in the third National Assembly. She pondered how to interact with her male colleagues and become accepted as their equal. Her personal strategies included the clothes she wore in her job as the only woman legislator. Kim Ch'ol-an decided to wear a pantsuit with a simple blouse, which served as a symbolic statement of sexual equality.

With the elected women legislators of the postrevolution era, bipolar images of political women emerge; the image of virtuous, conservative women on one end and that of an eccentric woman on the other end conforming completely to the masculine culture of political life.

Kim Yun-dok and Kim Chong-rye dressed in a slightly modified version of *hanbok*, implicitly conveying to the public the image of a traditional woman of virtue actively engaged in public life. The modified version has a shorter (usually ankle-length) and straighter skirt, and often the jacket is designed to be closed by an ornamental pin, while the classic style of women's clothes is a full floor-length wrap skirt and a short jacket to be closed by a long single-bow tie. When she was asked why she always wore *hanbok*, Kim Chong-rye extolled *hanbok* for being so comfortable and yet at the same time for being elegant and formal.

In stark contrast to her female colleagues, Kim Ok-son wears a man's suit and a necktie, which she regards as a kind of ritual robe, likening it to the robes worn by priests or judges. Her hair and footwear are also in men's styles. Even her masculine voice befits her look of a "dainty handsome man."[9]

The masculine appearance of Kim Ok-son was, of course, an idiosyncratic strategy but at the same time a most peculiarly culture-bound personal response to the systemic sexual discrimination based on the traditional gender-role ideology. Her transvestism underscores the transforming power of the combination of cultural forces and individual will over nature.

In Korea, female to male cross-dressing used to be imposed on young children by parents who expressed their ardent hopes of having a son for their next child. An autobiography of the "new woman" born around the turn of the century described the initial disappointment of her parents for having a female baby. However, her Christian mother was determined to give her young daughter formal education and sent the little "girl-son" to a nearby boys' school dressed in boy's clothes until the age of eight, when a new girls' school was built by Christian missionaries.[10] The parents of Pak Sun-ch'on, who was an only child, also dressed their daughter in boy's clothes when she was a young pupil among boys in a *sowon* (a private school where she learned Chinese classics).[11]

However, adult cross-dressing is extraordinary, and reactions to Kim Ok-son's transvestism are mixed. Some male members of her party at the national convention marveled at her mastery of masculine appearance with a mixture of admiration and curiosity (see the following section on professional activities). An old rural woman, who attended one of the homecoming reports of Representative Kim Ok-son in her constituency in Ch'ungch'ong province in September, 1985, exclaimed, "If only she possessed a pair of balls, she would be a complete man!" A journalist-turned-corporate executive said to me that although Kim Ok-son looked and sounded just like a man, he felt he found her femininity underneath the masculine facade when he held her soft supple hand in a handshake.

Kim Ch'ol-an's comment about Kim Ok-son's transvestism was sympathetic. She stated that Kim Ok-son could not have made it in her social environment without wearing pants. Indeed, Kim Ok-son herself stated that she had been severely criticized by the elder men of her province when she first began public life at the age of nineteen. In response, she started a "personal revolution" by dressing herself in men's attire out of her firm determination to play the role of son to her mother. For Kim Ok-son, the adoption of masculine appearance symbolized personal liberation from the shackles of the traditional gender-role system.[12]

Her transvestism has been a continuing source of journalistic curiosity ever since Kim Ok-son became the first *ch'onyo* (literally, virgin) legislator in 1968.[13] Newspaper and magazine articles never fail to mention her manly appearance. It was reported that some women tried to press her into discarding men's clothes after her first electoral victory, but Kim Ok-son declared that her decision to wear a man's suit was based on her philosophy of life and that she intended to show the world that men and women are truly equal in their potential by maintaining her masculine appearance until the end of her life.[14] Some of my informants refused to make comments about her transvestism, while others harshly criticized her for renouncing her female identity.

All appointed assemblywomen of the second generation wore Western-style clothes in their public lives. Many of them deliberately avoided wearing bright colors. One appointed assemblywoman was critical of Kim Yun-dok's strategy of wearing traditional clothes. She remembered an occasion when she and Kim Yun-dok traveled abroad together as members of the National Assembly. She stated that Kim Yun-dok looked charming in her stylish Western clothes during the trip and wondered with strong disapproval why she had to contrive her image by wearing traditional clothes in public life. (It should be noted here that Kim Yun-dok switched to Western-style clothes after being appointed to head the Korea Women's Development Institute in 1989.)[15]

Another appointed assemblywoman told me she had her shoulder-length hair cut shorter after her appointment, to look more dignified and professional. But, one of the former two-term appointed assemblywomen dared to challenge the popular notion that women politicians wore either traditional clothes or conservative suits. She did not hesitate to wear bell-bottoms when she felt like it. She made up her face, had her nails polished and sometimes wore conspicuous jewelry, such as dangling earrings. Her fashionably conspicuous appearance was frowned upon by some conservative people, who regarded it as inappropriate for a high public official.

Unlike some other Asian countries where both men and women customarily wear pants as well as skirts, Korean traditional custom has made pants a male garment and a skirt a female one. Hence, a woman's wearing pants, which may be interpreted as a sort of symbolic violation of the gender boundary, tends to offend the sensibility of more conservative Koreans. The negative reaction to the wearing of pants by a woman is a concrete example of the various conflicts caused by dual gender-role ideologies. The democratic ideology espouses sexual equality and personal freedom, while the traditional rules of conduct constrain women's lifestyles by prescribing gender-specific appearance and demeanor.

It has been suggested that members of a dominant culture group feel threatened by the presence of token representatives of a minority group because of (1) the danger that their dominant position may be overtaken and (2) the discomfort caused by a token's presence.[16] Even though Korean men need not worry over the danger of losing their dominant social position in the near future, they have been experiencing the discomfort of interacting with women in high office, both domestically and internationally. In general, these men seem to feel less uncomfortable and threatened by "feminine" women than by "masculine" women. In this regard, male voters may accept more readily those women politicians who project the image of virtuous, conservative women by wearing *hanbok* or Western-style feminine clothes of modest design than those "masculine" women wearing pants.

The acute sensitivity of women legislators to their proper outward appearance also stems from the traditional concept that the political elite govern others by their exemplary behavior.[17] A section chief in the city hall of Seoul paid me compliments for a reddish plaid jacket I wore during the interview. She said she did not dare to wear such a bright color to the office as a public official. A female judge informant in her early thirties, whom I met several times during my fieldwork, was always dressed in somber, sex-neutral colors such as gray, black, dark blue, and white. However, another female judge, a few years younger, not only wore a very feminine style of clothes but also had her nails done in a bright color. These different responses women in public life make to the pressures of dual gender-role ideologies seem to indicate a move toward a more pluralistic society where individuals may exhibit diverse attitudes and behaviors without risking social sanctions.

PROFESSIONAL ACTIVITIES

There are thirteen standing committees in the National Assembly, with

13
Comm.

the following functional designations: Legislation and Justice, Foreign Affairs, Home Affairs, Finance, Economy and Science, National Defense, Education and Public Information, Agriculture and Fisheries, Commerce and Industry, Health Affairs, Transportation and Communications, Construction, and Steering.

The committee assignments for women legislators were not limited to the "women's committees" such as Education or Health Affairs Committees. The eight women legislators of the twelfth National Assembly, for instance, were assigned to seven different committees. The two elected ones (Kim Ok-son and Kim Chong-rye) belonged to the National Defense and the Home Affairs Committees, respectively. The six appointed women members were assigned to the following five committees: Foreign Affairs (Kim Yong-chong), Economy and Science (Pak Hye-kyong), Education and Public Information (Kim Hyon-ja and Han Yang-sun), Commerce and Industry (Yang Kyong-ja), and Health Affairs (Kim Chang-suk).[18]

Despite their tiny minority status in the male-dominated National Assembly, elected women lawmakers—especially of the prerevolution era—were active in legislative life, concentrating on the areas most suited to their personal interests and talents.

Following her diplomatic activities in the United States, Yim Yong-sin focused on international relations, while Pak Sun-ch'on concentrated her efforts on laws advancing women's rights at workplaces as well as at home. Pak Sun-ch'on initiated bills concerning the right of working women to have a monthly day off and a sixty-day maternity leave with pay and a wife's equal right to sue an unfaithful spouse in case of adultery. When the latter bill was introduced, resistance from male legislators was strong: When it was voted into law by a margin of three votes, it was dubbed as the "Pak Sun-ch'on Law."[19]

In the case of Kim Ch'ol-an, she dared to run for the chair of the Social and Health Committee as a freshman lawmaker and the only female member of the third National Assembly. She said she did it not because it was important for her to become the chair, but because she wanted to demonstrate that a woman could do it. Accompanied by her husband, she campaigned by visiting the homes of the committee members late at night. To a surprised colleague who would suggest meeting in the office the following day, Kim Ch'ol-an said to me that she would reply, "I came to campaign to your wife!" She visited twenty-one colleagues in this manner during the week preceding the election. Then, on the day of the election, Kim Ch'ol-an told me that she paid a visit to her rival at his home at five o'clock in the morning. The assertive personal approach of her campaign proved to be effective, and in the end her competitor—a three-term veteran lawmaker—was so moved by Kim Ch'ol-an's sincerity, energy, and determination as to promise her that he would urge his followers to vote for Kim Ch'ol-an, whom he called *nunim* (elder sister). That morning, their colleagues were startled to see them arrive at the National Assembly riding in the same car.

Kim Ch'ol-an was elected by seventy-four to fifty votes to the chair of the Social and Health Committee of the third National Assembly, becoming the first and only committee chairwoman in the legislature. In thanking her colleagues, she made a deep "forty-five degree" bow to each of them and caught the hands of those who were unwilling to congratulate her in order to shake hands with them also.

The first issue she raised as the committee chair, despite the hostile attitude of many of her colleagues, was the allocation of funds for disabled veterans. Kim Ch'ol-an said that thousands of veterans who were gathered in front of the National Assembly building greeted her by raising their artificial steel hands high and calling her "mother" (*omoni*) in appreciation for her legislative efforts on their behalf.

In comparison, legislative actions of women legislators of the post-revolution era have been less conspicuous or memorable, except in the case of Kim Ok-son.

Kim Ok-son is unique among the women legislators not only because she has never married and always wears men's clothes but also because her political career has been unusually rough and dramatic. She is the only woman legislator who claimed her legislative seat by waging a legal battle against the fraudulent election of her opponent. Furthermore, she is the only woman lawmaker who has been forced to resign from the National Assembly, compelled to do so because of the ire she caused President Park with her critical speech on dictatorship during a regular session in the National Assembly.

Her critical speech on the "dictatorial regime" on October 8, 1975—as mentioned briefly in Chapter 4—was interrupted abruptly in the middle of delivery and brought about a political storm. Her criticism of the Park regime was based on the opposition party platform for the 1975 legislative session. Her colleagues and the party leadership, however, failed to support her when the ruling party adamantly insisted on punishing her by dismissing her from the legislature, for she violated the "sacred precincts" (*songyok*) of taboo subjects by questioning the legitimacy of the Park regime's policies.[20]

On the morning of October 13, after she had had a visit with Kim Yong-sam, the leader of the New Democratic Party (Sinmindang), at his house the previous evening, Kim Ok-son had to submit her resignation from the National Assembly in accordance with the advice from the leader of her party,[21] which ended the "Kim Ok-son *p'adong* (crisis)" five days after her fateful speech.[22]

After her resignation, Kim Ok-son was indicted for a violation of election laws by having a rally during the 1972 presidential election campaign without a prior notice to authorities. She was sentenced to one year's imprisonment and two year's stay of execution. All her civic rights were suspended for eight years. Kim Ok-son said that she had to "live like a vegetable." She became "a fish out of water" until she was returned to the National Assembly in 1985 after ten years' forced absence from the political arena.

In the twelfth National Assembly, Kim Ok-son concentrated her legislative work on the issues of national security and defense. On behalf of the New Korea Democratic Party, Kim Ok-son introduced to her legislative colleagues in the Steering Committee "a resolution for a parliamentary investigation to verify the Kwangju incident" in June, 1985.[23] She was credited for having handled the explosive issue of the Kwangju incident gracefully and persuasively.[24]

Kim Ok-son then ran for the vice-chair of her party at the special convention of the New Korea Democratic Party in August, 1985. I was able to attend the convention at her invitation and observed the heated processes of power games played by about eight hundred delegates of a major opposition party. Kim Ok-son was nominated on the slate of six candidates for the three vice-chair positions, but last-minute factional politics between the two Kim cliques prevented her from winning the election. One of the candidates for the vice-chair (Sin To-hwan) made a surprise announcement when the meeting reconvened after lunch that he would relinquish his candidacy to his colleague (No Sung-hwan). The delegates were supposed to vote for three vice-chairs but many of them wrote in four names at the "secret instruction" of their faction leaders. They had to vote again to select only three.

The process of electing vice-chairs took the whole afternoon plus evening hours in the smoke-filled, crowded hall at the old National Assembly building on a sultry August day. Kim Ok-son campaigned tirelessly during the marathon race for the vice-chair delivering an impassioned speech, making rounds throughout the hall, and getting hearty applause from the sections where the delegates from Ch'ungch'ong province were seated.

A Mr. Cho, a delegate of over sixty years of age from Kyongsang province who sat two seats away from me, commented to his young neighbor, a Mr. Kwon, that Kim Ok-son behaved so perfectly like a man. He also added that she must have never worn a bra in her life; it seemed that these men recognized her as a full-fledged politician but could not help being reminded of the fact that she is a woman. Cho said that he felt sympathetic toward her for she was the only woman (*hongilchom*).

When the candidates began their final rounds of campaigning before the second voting, Kwon half-jestingly suggested to his neighbor that he should vote for her, to which Cho replied, "Of course! I already voted for her, for she is *namjang yogol* (a heroic woman dressed in man's clothes)." (See Chapter 8 on the concept of *yogol*.) Even though a considerable number (267) of the 680 delegates voted for Kim Ok-son—who was regarded to be the forerunner among the independents who wanted to check the rampant factionalism based on the regional origins of the two leaders of the main rival factions[25]—she was unable to win the race against the forces of the main factions.

Two months later, when the death of Vice-Speaker Kim Nok-yong of the New Korea Democratic Party brought about a house election for the vacant vice-speakership (which was slotted for the main opposition party), Kim Ok-son decided to run independently in defiance of the party leadership. Her frustration and dissatisfaction with the intraparty factional politics prompted her to compete for the post against her party nominee Yi Yong-hi, who was recommended by a factional leader Kim Dae-jung.[26] Two more legislators (Pak Hae-ch'ung and Cho Yon-ha) from her party also ran for the vice-speakership in defiance of their party decision to support Representative Yi Yong-hi.

Kim Ok-son won the support of 34 of the 102 fellow legislators from her party, but was unable to win the race, which required the support of more than half of the total membership. She not only lost the election but was punished by the party with a suspension of her membership for two years. (The two-year suspension of party membership was also placed on Cho Yon-ha, who won the election by defeating the party nominee Yi Yong-hi in the second round of voting. Pak Hae-ch'ung was reprimanded for his rebellious action by the Executive Council of the party.)[27] When her colleagues were deliberating a final punitive measure for her disobedient action on January 30, 1986, Kim Ok-son—who was herself a member of the Executive Council—was out of the country to attend the national breakfast prayer meeting for President Reagan in Washington, D.C.

Kim Yun-dok asserted that she was one of the three most active lawmakers of the ninth National Assembly and that her legislative activities were concerned mainly with family and health problems. Kim Chong-rye seemed most concerned about the welfare of the needy people in her constituency. I observed her visits to old people's homes and a home for the disabled in late December, 1985. She comforted them and offered gifts of coal briquettes for the former groups and stockings for the latter as tokens of her concern for their welfare.

It is in the area of legislative activities that appointed women legislators in general feel especially powerless. In fact, the problem is not unique to them but is shared by their male counterparts, because the major role of an appointed legislator is to serve the party by endorsing party policies unconditionally. This aspect of the political function of appointed legislators is caricatured by the pejorative nickname *kosugi* (hand-raising machine), to describe appointed lawmakers who raise their hands to vote in agreement with all the policy decisions of party leaders.[28] They have played an integral part in rubber-stamping government-proposed legislation.[29]

The general impression, however, is that appointed legislators of the opposition party have more autonomy than their counterparts in the ruling party. The fact that the former made substantial contributions to party funds for their appointments makes their position in the party more autonomous than the latter group, who owe absolute obedience to the head of the party in return for his favor of appointing them to the legislature.

Nonetheless, Pak Hyon-suk, as an appointed member of the ruling party at the sixth National Assembly, made a notable and rare exception in asserting her stance against her party's position by abstaining from voting for the normalization of Korea-Japan diplomatic relations in 1965. Having personally experienced cruel persecution by the Japanese during colonial rule, Pak Hyon-suk could not find room in her heart to trust the sincerity of the Japanese people in this diplomatic gesture.[30] In her case, there is no doubt that the prestige of being a well-known, respected pioneer political woman in her sixties enabled her to assert her position without fear of a political reprisal for her independent action.

The relative lack of autonomy for appointed members of the National Assembly in the legislative process was clearly underlined when the eleventh National Assembly failed to endorse a bill concerning revision of the Family Law. All the appointed female members from the ruling party voted against it, in accordance with party policy, although they were personally in favor of revising the Family Law.

Another source of structural constraint for appointed assemblywomen in their professional activities is the lack of legitimacy of the proportional representation party list system itself in the minds of many people. Negative perception of the system is rather widespread. Some of the university students in my survey, for example, felt strongly enough to write on their own that the system should be abolished, even though the questionnaire required only marking a choice among the multiple answers. But one appointed woman legislator who had formerly been a professor vindicated the proportional party list system and likened her fellow appointed legislators to the members of the upper house of the parliament in other countries.

However, some appointed women legislators compared their positions to those of "illegitimate children" (*soja*). They are aware of the negative perception of the proportional representation party list system by the general public, as well as of their "accessory" positions within the appointive system. In the ninth National Assembly, for instance, there were ten appointed assemblywomen, but only one was allowed an opportunity to make a formal speech in the National Assembly. In this context, it is not surprising that many appointed assemblywomen opt for adaptive responses of a predictably passive nature, avoiding being conspicuous and following the party line faithfully. Indeed, party affiliations seemed a major variable for the leadership styles of women legislators. Those belonging to the ruling party seemed to stress the images of civic-minded, virtuous, and caring women, while those belonging to the opposition camp appeared to emphasize the images of heroic fighters for true democracy. Chapter 8 discusses the various leadership styles and images that women legislators of Korea present to the public.

NOTES

1. For example, see Vallance (1979) for the experiences of British women politicians.

2. For a discussion of "the supremacy of personal and private considerations in South Korean politics," see Han (1974:74-76). See also Kim and Cho (1972); Han (1984).

3. Yim (1951:296).

4. *Chosun Ilbo*, February 27, 1972.

5. Janelli and Janelli (1982:65).

6. The Women's Police Station was abolished in 1957 (KWA 1986:30).

7. Y. Kim (1979).

8. For more details concerning Korean dress, see Soh (1992).

9. *Han'guk Ilbo*, February 23, 1985.

10. Pahk (1954).

11. K. Kim (1984).

12. *Taehan Ilbo*, June 11, 1968; Yun (1985).

13. *Chosun Ilbo*, June 4, 1968; *Taehan Ilbo*, June 11, 1968.

14. *Han'guk Ilbo*, June 9, 1968.

15. During my meeting with her in January 1990, Kim Yun-dok, dressed in Western-style clothes, stated that people at the Institute felt uncomfortable with her wearing *hanbok*, interpreting it as authoritarian behavior. Since most women now wear Western-style clothes in public, wearing *hanbok* generated a rather inappropriate effect for her new role as the head of a progressive research institute dedicated to improving women's status. Her experience underscores the connection between dress and social status: Change in social position demands a change in dress style (Bean 1989; Stone 1965).

16. Kanter (1977).

17. See Pye (1985) for a discussion of the Confucian concept of power and leadership.

18. *Han'guk Ilbo*, May 16, 1985; NA (1985).

19. Pak (1974-75:32).

20. For more discussion of *songyok*, see Kang (1988).

21. For the detrimental effect of the Kim Ok-son *p'adong* on the political life of Kim Yong-sam, see So (1984).

22. O. Kim (1984); Om (1986).

23. *Han'guk Ilbo*, June 6, 1985.

24. Yun (1985).

25. *Chugan Han'guk*, pp. 20-25, April 28, 1985.

26. For more details on her decision to run for the vice-speaker, see O. Kim (1985).

27. *Korea Times*, December 28, 1985.

28. H. Kim (1975:157).

29. H. Kim (1975; 1977); Han (1984:264).

30. SPC (1968:440-43).

8

Private Meanings and Public Images

Almost all male Korean lawmakers proudly adorn the lapels of their jackets with a gold badge that signifies their membership in the National Assembly. The gold badge, which is shaped in the form of a hibiscus (the national flower) and has the Chinese character *kuk* (nation) inscribed in the center (see Figure 8.1), is a precious symbol of political power and social status.

Figure 8.1
The Badge for Legislators

During an interview conducted when she was returned to the National Assembly after ten years' forced absence from the political arena, Kim Ok-son was wearing the gold badge. Her friend asked Representative Kim whether it was an old one. Kim Ok-son replied that she had been given a new one and that she felt a little self-conscious and bashful wearing it after such a long absence, even though she felt that nobody else deserved it more than she did. Her friend then advised Representative Kim that she should preserve her old gold badge in a picture frame.[1]

For Koreans, becoming a member of the National Assembly not only signals a professional success for the individual but also enhances social prestige for the lawmaker's whole family. I was told, for instance, that a newly elected legislator in the twelfth National Assembly presented his gold badge at the tomb of his deceased father as he took a proud bow to his ancestors to share the honor he brought to the family. However, some women legislators—especially the appointed ones—said that they avoided wearing their gold badges. Why?

A study of male legislators reported that "extrinsic" rewards (such as personal prestige, career opportunities, and material well-being) motivated an overwhelming majority (83 percent) of males to become lawmakers.[2] What about their female counterparts? What meaning do the women of this study give to their lives as legislators?

THE MEANING OF A LEGISLATIVE CAREER

The consideration of the social prestige of the *chiban* (clan)[3] appeared as an important aspect in the meaning of the political careers of Kim Ch'ol-an and Kim Ok-son and, to some degree, Yim Yong-sin, as well. The concept of *chiban*, in comparison with that of *munjung* (lineage), is more inclusive in that it includes relatives who are not related agnatically. Thus, the Korean concept of *chiban* is comparable to Murdock's definition of the clan, a "compromise kin group" that is based upon both a rule of residence and a rule of descent.[4]

Let us look at the case of Kim Ch'ol-an, in which the whole *chiban* participated in the process of deciding she should run for a legislative seat.

Kim Ch'ol-an is a tall and energetic woman with a very fair complexion. Her imposing physical appearance[5] fitted well the traditional image of the "first daughter-in-law of a wealthy family." Her husband's family was *mansokkun*, which may be translated as "millionaire," although the expression literally means a person or family who possesses ten thousand *sok* (51,200 U.S. bushels) of grain.

By the time Liberation came, Kim Ch'ol-an had borne four children and had firmly established herself as a trustworthy daughter-in-law to her affinal parents. Kim then was the chairwoman of the Patriotic Women's Association (Aeguk Puinhoe). Her reputation as a generous, able matron must have been very high, for the all-male village association of Confucians recommended that her father-in-law (who headed the association) let her represent their community in the first National Assembly election.

Her father-in-law convened a family meeting to discuss the matter and to decide who should run in the election to represent their *chiban* as well as their village. The family agreed that Kim Ch'ol-an was the best candidate for the task at hand, and her husband strongly supported the idea.

Her husband and male relatives worked together in her election campaign, and the family spent a sizable amount of their wealth to finance her campaign. Kim Ch'ol-an related that the family spent seven hundred *sok* (one *sok* or *som* equals 5.12 U.S. bushels) out of their *mansok* (ten thousand *sok*) of rice to finance her campaign. This is saying that they spent about seven percent of the family wealth for her election.

Her son, a professor of law, told me that his mother used to explain to him and his sisters that her involvement in politics was in accordance with the wishes of his grandfather as well as his father. If the children did not behave themselves during her absence and became troublemakers, she would quit her political life immediately to return to full-time motherhood. The son added that the activities of his *chiban* revolved around his mother while she was a legislator.

What, then, motivated a conservative old man in a rural town to endorse a political career for his daughter-in-law? What I suggest here is that the father-in-law, in allowing Kim Ch'ol-an to pursue a legislative seat, was utilizing the talents of a member of his *chiban* to enhance the social prestige of his *chiban*. Kim Ch'ol-an, as an affinal member of the Ch'oe *chiban*, could bring social honor to it by becoming a legislator.

The behavior of the menfolk of Kim Ch'ol-an's *chiban* exemplifies the adaptationist attitude based on traditional familial values. It is an adaptive response to the dialectics of dual gender-role ideologies. On the surface it appears to embrace the modern democratic ideology of sexual equality for Kim Ch'ol-an, but it is deeply rooted in traditional values of social prestige of the *chiban* and moral excellence of its individual members.

A manifestation of the adaptationist attitude at the individual level is the belief held by Kim Ch'ol-an and many other women of this study—which is shared by most men—that the fulfilling of traditional feminine roles and leading of a virtuous personal life are prerequisites for a woman's entry into the political arena. In other words, a new role for women in politics is added to the traditional set of women's roles, without bringing about fundamental changes in the traditional gender-role system. Furthermore, the endorsement of a woman's pursuit of a political career by patriarchal authority figures (such as fathers, fathers-in-law, or husbands) functions as an unassailable legitimation for her to cross the traditional boundary of the gender-role system. The idea of sexual equality was only implicitly and inconspicuously a basis of her public career.

At the group level, the social prestige of *chiban* is at the root of the adaptationist attitude, as stated earlier. In order to understand the full implications of the statement, however, we need to consider the importance Koreans attach to social prestige. A most telling example of Korean's concern for status is the organizational characteristics of the Korean lineage, such as the existence of large national-level agnatic organizations with which local lineages affiliate to back their claims to status and the importance of illustrious ancestry rather than wealth as the basis for an internal segmentation of a lineage.[6] The main functions of the Korean lineage organization have been ancestor worship and the promotion of its own status by glorifying the ancestors' prestige.[7]

In traditional Korea, it was by becoming a scholar-official that one could achieve social status and wealth. In modern Korea, politicians still rank highest in occupational prestige,[8] and politics is regarded as one of the most effective channels of social mobility, for "it confers prestige, status, power, and even wealth."[9]

Thus, male members of some *chiban* and lineage organizations have reconciled the conflicting dual gender-role ideologies by recognizing new opportunities for them to enhance their social prestige through endorsing a female member of their group to enter the male-dominated field of politics.[10] The encouragement by men of potentially successful women to run for office or to play other political roles can thus be seen as a newly added strategy in the age-old concern for enhancing the welfare of the *chiban*.

In the case of Kim Ok-son, whose public life began at the age of nineteen when she opened a home for war-stricken widows and orphans in her home town of Changhang in South Ch'ungch'ong province, it was at the urging of her *chiban* elders (the Kwangsan Kims) that she decided to run in the fifth National Assembly election after the demise of the Rhee regime. The lineage elders chose Kim Ok-son to represent the Kim *chiban* and enhance their social prestige by her becoming a legislator. This endorsement of a young woman's quest for a legislative seat by the lineage elders in a very conservative region of the country was another example of the adaptationist attitude, adopting the modern gender-role ideology out of their desire to promote the social prestige of their *chiban*.

At the personal level, Kim Ok-son seemed to have regarded her professional success in politics as a fulfillment of her filial duty to her mother, who had wholeheartedly backed her daughter psychologically and financially. She prided herself for being perhaps the only truly self-made female politician.

Yim Yong-sin also appeared to have felt about her political career a similar sense of fulfillment of filial duty to her father. When Yim Yong-sin returned to Korea in August, 1948, after successfully accomplishing her diplomatic mission at the United Nations (see Chapter 5), her seventy-six-year-old father was among the enthusiastic crowd waiting at the airport to welcome her back. The placard carried by the faculty and staff of her Chungang University read: "Long live Yim Yong-sin, Korea's Joan of Arc."[11]

Upon arrival at home, Yim offered a "big bow" (*k'unjol*) to her father and asked him, "Do you still wish I were born a boy?" (He had commented, when she was young, that Yong-sin should have been born a boy, and that as such, he would have made it in one way or another, either as a government official or a gangster.) The joyous father answered, "I am proud to have a distinguished daughter like you in our *Yim-ssi chiban* (the Yim clan). You are a worthy offspring who has brought illustrious honor to our *Yim-ssi chiban*."[12]

This was the father who had flogged little Yong-sin for violating the parental role expectations of an obedient daughter and had tried to marry her off before she reached her teens. However, by the time Yong-sin returned to Korea to a hero's welcome for her diplomatic accomplishments, her father clearly had changed his outlook on gender-role performance and had taken an adaptationist attitude to regard his daughter's achievement as the enhancement of the social prestige of his *chiban*.

Today, even a woman with a history of divorce can be treated with a titular honor in the lineage association when she achieves professional success and social fame at the national level. One such legislator has been accorded the honor of vice-president in her lineage association. The majority of lineage associations, however, are not so progressive. Some men of more conservative lineages were offended by the violation of the patrilineal principle in the above-mentioned lineage association and made disparaging remarks that the lineage in question did not belong to the *yangban* class.

Kim Ok-son, as a three-term legislator, was honored as president of the Kwangsan Kim Lineage Association. These examples, while still very rare, are precious evidence of the adaptationist attitude held by some men, resulting in a positive move toward structural change in the gender-role system.

Although the personal meanings of political careers vary according to the individuals, they seemed to have been significantly influenced by historical events and circumstances that women of this study experienced during their adolescence. For instance, pioneer-generation political women, who grew up as the educational elite of their society under the Japanese occupation, appeared to have felt a strong moral obligation to use their education for social and political causes. Indeed, it was their genuinely patriotic sense of mission rather than personal desires for extrinsic rewards that seemed to characterize pioneer-generation women legislators' motivation for active political participation both before and after liberation from the Japanese colonial rule.

As for the women legislators of the postrevolution era, differences in their motivations for political participation divide them into two groups: (1) those who voluntarily joined a political party and/or ran for the National Assembly and (2) those who were appointed to the legislature without having aspired to active political participation. The first group may be identified as true "political women," which includes all the elected women legislators plus a few appointed ones. Most of appointed women legislators belonged to the second group, the "political appointees."

Kim Yun-dok, as a "political woman," took a special pride in having done it all——fulfilling traditional women's roles and actively participating in the tough male-dominated world of politics. But she was ambivalent about her career in the opposition camp. She was proud of herself for having been a loyal oppositionist but at the same time thought that her affiliation with the opposition party delimited the boundary of her activities and influence. When I met her in 1985, she was a full-time housewife who was still deeply concerned about politics and looking for meaningful ways to be involved in public life. In February, 1989, she was appointed to head the Korea Women's Development Institute.

Kim Chong-rye also appeared to feel a sense of achievement for having carried out both traditional women's roles and new public roles for women in modern society. The few appointed political women also showed pride in their active participation in national politics. The current members of the twelfth National Assembly belonging to this group, for example, did not fail to wear their gold badges.

In contrast, the "political appointees," who seemed to regard their political participation as a fulfillment of honorable civic duty, avoided wearing their gold badges. They made it a point not to wear the gold badge especially when they met their former colleagues or went to the meetings at women's organizations, lest they appear boastful and provoke envy and/or resentment in their former colleagues. One of them said that her children are proud of her but at the same time very wary of the negative perceptions by some people of the appointed legislators and of the ruling party.

For the political appointees in general, different occupational backgrounds seemed an important variable to affect individual perspectives on their legislative lives. For those professors of political science who were able to return to their university positions after the one-term legislative service, their experiences in the legislature were useful and unique episodes in their professional lives. They felt they benefited from having participated in the real world of politics, about which they taught and theorized. One of them pointed to the expansion of her social network as a specific advantage of having been a legislator. She further stated that although she recognized the importance of having more women participate in national politics and admired the few elected women legislators, she would not want to become a politician because it was still too rough an occupation for women under the present social and political circumstances.

For the assemblywomen who came from women's organizations——the majority of whom were in their fifties——their experiences as legislators offered valuable training in political socialization. One of them confessed that at the start of her legislative career she had only the vaguest idea what the National Assembly was all about but felt well prepared to embark on a political career by the time her first term expired. Her case illustrates a positive effect of actual participation of women in political life on enhancing their political consciousness and generating ambitions for a political career. (The above-mentioned informant was given the opportunity to serve in the legislature again as an appointed member of the ruling party in the thirteenth National Assembly.) Another appointed woman in the eleventh National Assembly said that becoming a politician had been her childhood dream but that she became very disappointed with political life after her participation in the legislature and decided to go back to her legal career.

One of the practical gains of becoming lawmakers, which most appointed women legislators seemed to appreciate quietly but would rather not talk about, was an increase in their income and various perquisites that accompanied their appointments. At least two former women's organization leaders frankly expressed their appreciation of their legislative appointments in this respect.

The length of service was another factor that influenced the attitudes of appointed assemblywomen toward being a legislator. A writer who served as an appointed member in the tenth National Assembly, which lasted for only a year, felt that her appointive tenure in the legislature was all too short for her to feel a sense of accomplishment as a legislator. It made her feel ambivalent about revealing her brief stint as a legislator in her resume.

In general, legislative appointments for women are a one-term honor; this is a source of frustration for the "political women" but of relief for most "political appointees." For example, a former director of the Women's Bureau of a political party who was in her forties felt frustrated at the anticipated lack of further opportunities to continue her legislative career once her one-term appointment was over. She said that her husband and sons were very proud of her professional involvement in national politics and intimated that she would exert her utmost to merit a multiple-term service in the legislature. Three years after our interview, she was reappointed to serve in the thirteenth National Assembly.

Negative aspects of being an assemblywoman mentioned by women of this study included the "celebrity tax" they had to pay and the burden they had to shoulder of representing the female population. Since appointed women legislators are expected to focus their energy on resolving women's issues, they are subject to group pressures from formal women's organizations. However, as described in Chapter 7, under the prevailing social and political circumstances there is little that appointed women legislators can actually do on their own to fulfill their obligation to represent women's interests. Not surprisingly, a comparative study found that Korean female legislators feel more role strain at representing the female population than do the congresswomen of the United States.[13]

TYPES AND IMAGES

The women legislators I have studied are few in number but diverse in their occupational backgrounds, gender-role ideologies, motivations, and patterns of political participation. They also exhibited marked differences in their leadership styles, covering the whole spectrum from a low-profile receptive one to a charismatic vanguard.

On the basis of their gender-role performance in both public and private spheres, I have divided them into two major categories: neotraditionalist and vanguard. The neotraditionalists fulfill traditional feminine roles and divide their lives into public and private domains. The vanguards refuse to follow the paths of traditional feminine life and pursue their life goals as independent women. These two basic types can be further subdivided according to leadership styles and the meaning political careers appeared to hold for them, producing the following four images of Korean female legislators in the past four decades: the Virtuous Woman, the Nurturing Woman, the Heroic Woman, and the Self-Actualized Woman (see Table 8.1).

Many appointed and some elected women legislators presented images of the modern Virtuous Woman, regarding their political participation as fulfillment of their civic duty, and acting in a modest, receptive manner. Some elected women legislators seemed to view their role in political life as the extension of their traditional gender role to take care of people and presented images of the compassionately Nurturing Woman. Some appointed women legislators projected images of a Self-Actualized Woman. They seemed to regard their legislative appointments as the recognition of their professional achievements and took on their new job in a businesslike manner. A few elected women legislators presented images of the Heroic Woman, plunging into the political arena with a wholehearted devotion and pioneering through untrodden paths with charisma.

Of course, not all political women fit into these four categories perfectly. Some women who on the surface look like Virtuous Women share the mundane motivation of self-aggrandizement and imitate the authoritarian behavior of their male counterparts. Other Virtuous Women reveal nurturing attitudes and heroically selfless behavior in their roles as lawmakers. One woman classified here as a Nurturing Woman has also exhibited the qualities of a Heroic Woman in her leadership behavior. This typology of political women is an overview of the *patterns of adaptive response* women legislators have made in carrying out their nontraditional

Table 8.1
Types and Images of Korean Women Legislators

TYPE	Neotraditionalist		Vanguard	
Traditional Gender-Role Performance	Yes		No	
Public/Private Role Polarization	Yes		No	
IMAGE	Virtuous Woman	Nurturing Woman	Self-Actualized Woman	Heroic Woman
Meaning of Political Career	Civic duty	Feminine care	Professional recognition	Wholehearted dedication
Leadership Style	Receptive	Compassionate	Businesslike	Charismatic

roles under the pressure of dual gender-role ideologies in Korean society. It is not a rigorous typology of the women themselves.

The Virtuous Woman

The Virtuous Woman regards the traditional feminine role as her primary responsibility and fulfills her wifely and motherly duties. She handles the conflicting sets of gender-role ideologies by polarizing her life into public and private domains. She advocates women's rights in public life but accepts the traditional sexual division of labor at home as natural. A legislative career to her means an honorable "civic duty" to perform. Her appearance is in line with the proper styles of the times. She keeps a low profile in the political arena. It is important for her to maintain a good social reputation as a woman of traditional feminine virtues. The majority of appointed and some elected women legislators of this study presented images of the Virtuous Woman.

The leadership behavior of the Virtuous Woman is based on the stereotypic female model: cooperative and receptive rather than competitive and aggressive. Pak Sun-ch'on suffered from a chronic kidney disease, which, it was believed, was caused by the lack of a women's restroom facility in the old National Assembly building. Instead of demanding that a women's restroom be installed, Pak Sun-ch'on tried her patience and her kidney while she attended the legislative sessions. She also tried to limit her intake of beverages to a minimum and avoided having soup at her meal while the National Assembly was in session.

The leadership style of Pak Sun-ch'on as the head of the opposition party is a good example of the Virtuous Woman style. After the military revolution, Pak Sun-ch'on took the helm of the newly formed Democratic Party (Minjudang) at the request of her colleagues in 1963. She never actively sought to be the leader of her party; instead she was asked to lead the party by those members who respected her skills and integrity as a politician. She did not wish to take the position, but accepted the nomination with the desire to help unite the opposing factions among her colleagues under her leadership.[14] She suspected that one of the major reasons the men asked her to lead the party was their awareness of women voters, which made her very self-conscious and more careful about her own behavior as a woman.[15]

Pak Sun-ch'on longed for clean politics and was critical of the many questionable ways in which political funds were raised by her male colleagues, yet she did not attempt to remedy the situation.[16] She thought that more women in politics would help decrease corruption,[17] but did little to encourage or sponsor female political aspirants. She stated that she was "not a smart politician" because she stubbornly tried to apply her personal principles to politics.[18]

Pak Sun-ch'on, as president of the Democratic People's Party (Minjungdang)[19] tried to avoid the deadlock in the legislature over the restoration of diplomatic relations with Japan and the sending of Korean troops to Vietnam by meeting with President Park in July, 1965. When the agreement made between her and President Park on the procedural matters to resolve the political issues was announced, the hardliners within her party denounced it harshly. Pak Sun-ch'on was appalled at the misunderstanding of her sincere intentions, but did not——or perhaps could not——do much to prevent the factional strife and the eventual breakup of her party. About a year and half later, a unified opposition New Democratic Party (Sinmindang) was formed, and Pak Sun-ch'on handed over the leadership post. She retired from political life in December, 1972.

After her retirement, Pak Sun-ch'on developed a friendly relationship with the first lady, Yuk Yong-su (Mrs. Park Chung Hee), who sought the advice and friendship of the veteran woman politician. Many of her former colleagues and admirers in the opposition camp were shocked at the relationship and regarded it as a sellout of the lifelong opposition party figure. Pak Sun-ch'on on her part seemed at first incredulous of such criticism, which left her bitter and disenchanted with political life. She stated that she should have stayed in social work but strayed into politics and led an unusual life for a woman.[20]

The Nurturing Woman

The Nurturing Woman, like the Virtuous Woman, is also married and has children. Nevertheless, she takes a different, more pragmatic perspective on her traditional female role than the Virtuous Woman. She recognizes the functional value of the fulfillment of traditional feminine role performance as a crucial social resource for her public life. Kim Ch'ol-an, for example, stated that marital life and childbirth experiences are necessary ingredients to make a woman's public life a success. She attributed her successful public life to her good luck in having the right kind of man for a husband.

In her legislator's role, the Nurturing Woman takes a more assertive posture than the Virtuous Woman. She actively seeks to create a synthesis out of the contradictions generated by the dual gender-role ideologies. Hence, when she wears a man's suit, she replaces a man's white shirt and tie with a woman's colorful blouse, as shown in the case of Kim Ch'ol-an. If she wears a traditional costume, as in the case of Kim Chong-rye, it is a modernized version rather than an original form (which is ill suited for active life). Her leadership behavior revolves around the theme of feminine care and "maternal love." It evokes in the minds of men images of an elder sister (*nuna*), a mother (*omoni*), or a grandmother (*halmoni*).

Kim Ch'ol-an is the prime example of a Nurturing Woman. Her nurturing leadership style was amply demonstrated in various episodes during the Korean War, as described in Chapter 5. Even during her imprisonment after the fifth general election in 1960 (see Chapter 6), she found a way to conduct "charitable business" for her fellow inmate, a former spy. Every Friday, Kim Ch'ol-an would give the inmate some money so that she could buy herself rice cakes. She would also provide the former spy with clothing such as underwear.

When Kim Ch'ol-an was the only woman member in the third National Assembly, she helped arrange a goodwill baseball tournament between the ruling and opposition parties. After the game, while her male colleagues were enjoying a dance party at Chosun Hotel, Kim Ch'ol-an decided to make an unofficial visit to the nearby "Chongsam" street, a red-light district in Seoul, to assess the prostitution situation.

Dressed in baseball attire with a cap on, Kim Ch'ol-an went to Chongsam pretending to be a man. Seated in a small shabby room, she recognized the voice of a man in the next room; he was one of the National Assembly correspondents who had earlier in the day covered the sporting event. The politician's voice in her told her not to waste this opportunity. Embarrassed to be found there, the journalist told Kim Ch'ol-an, "It is a plus for you but a minus for me [for us to meet here]. I promise to write well of you." Kim Ch'ol-an prodded him to do charitable work and help her "buy the young girls out" of prostitution. Kim Ch'ol-an and the correspondent collected about ninety thousand *hwan* between them.[21] They were about thirty or forty thousand *hwan* short, but were able to rescue seven young women with that money by telling the owner that they worked at the National Assembly. She left them in the custody of a woman police chief that night.

The following day she enlisted the help of the minister of health and social welfare and had the women receive free medical treatment for venereal disease before sending them home with some money. Kim Ch'ol-an told them that after they returned home they should not mention their shameful lives in Seoul to anyone, but work hard, get married, and come visit her with a child. She said that a few years later one of them indeed came to see her on Ch'usok (a Korean thanksgiving day, which falls on the eighth full moon of the year) with a child on her back and a gift box of persimmons. The whole episode earned Kim Ch'ol-an the nickname of "mother-in-law" (*changmo*).

Another anecdote again illustrates her nurturing leadership style. When a thief awakened her in the middle of the night with a flashlight, Kim Ch'ol-an's immediate response was to apologize to him for not having taken good care of the people's livelihood. She then bade him to take whatever he wanted, or to come see her at her office in the National Assembly the next day. After a moment's deliberation, the thief rushed out of sight. When he showed up in her office the following morning, he confessed that he was not a professional thief, that he was formerly a school teacher transferred to Seoul from Koch'ang in South Kyongsang province but had recently been fired, that his wife had just delivered a baby, and that he had no money to feed the family. After hearing his problems, Kim Ch'ol-an called the minister of agriculture, who was also from Koch'ang, and through his help, found the man employment with a company dealing in agricultural chemicals. Kim Ch'ol-an said that the man came back in three days to pay her a formal visit and express his heartfelt gratitude with a bundle of flowers. She added that "nobody is a born thief," and that it was all a matter of "giving *chong* (compassion)."

The Self-Actualized Woman

Psychologists have indicated that the need for self-actualization is at the top of the hierarchy of human needs and that "man's tendency to actualize himself, to become his potentialities" leads to a high degree of creativity.[22] The third image of Korean political woman, which typically characterizes unmarried appointed women legislators, is the Self-Actualized Woman, the modern professional woman who cherishes her autonomy and self-development. She values the freedom of single life while recognizing the importance of marriage for social and psychological reasons. She does not feel bound to fulfill traditional feminine roles and quietly leads an independent life as a career woman seeking self-actualization. If she married and her marriage did not work, she would rather end it than either pretend it was a good marriage or patiently put up with a bad one. She is aware of the general disapproval of such a life-style, and it is part of her survival strategy to shun publicity.

An example of a Self-Actualized Woman is a "political administrator" (see Chapter 6) who is the eldest daughter raised in a father-absent family. She led an active student life as class leader and student union president and knew that she would have to work to help her mother financially. Despite her interest in fine arts, therefore, she chose law because she thought it would be of more use to her in leading a working woman's life.

Upon her graduation from the prestigious Law School of Seoul National University, she started as a newspaper reporter and covered social affairs for several years before her recruitment into the Democratic Republican Party. Her ability and hard work were rewarded by rapid promotions. She became a deputy director of the Bureau of Organizational Affairs at the age of thirty-five. Some men were jealous and felt uncomfortable working under a young female boss. As a symbolic gesture of boycott, the men tried to move her desk out of their bureau into the Women's Bureau, but my informant resolutely confronted them, indicating that it was not just a matter affecting her as an individual but concerning order in the workplace. Once she overcame the crisis, she was able to keep things under control.

After she was appointed to the eighth National Assembly, she felt the need to know more about economics and took up business administration at a graduate school. People interpreted her behavior as an ambitious strategy to strengthen her political career. After about four years' life as a legislator, however, she practically retired. The formal reason she gave me for her early retirement was that she was exhausted from having wholeheartedly exerted all her efforts in each phase of her professional life and that she needed a rest. However, a woman journalist (who had also served in the legislature as an appointed member) expressed her sympathy and regrets that the talents of her former colleague were being wasted due to the particular political climate in Korea.

It is difficult to assess her leadership behavior as a legislator or politician because appointed assemblywomen are at the bottom of the leadership hierarchy and as such are seldom given an opportunity even to address the National Assembly formally. Having spent all her adult life competing among men——going to a coed university and working among newspaper reporters, political party members, and legislators——she believes that there is no sex difference in abilities and performs her tasks in a businesslike manner. She does not deny her female identity or try to exploit it for her professional success. She remembered how her former boss——a newspaper editor——advised her to minimize femininity to be an effective journalist. (As Kanter pointed out, the minimization of sexual attributes is a characteristic response that token women often make to the performance pressure of her male-dominated workplace.)[23]   At the time of the interview, I noticed that she wore no makeup and had a short and simple hairstyle; the color of her clothes was beige, and her manner was unassuming and straightforward.

My informant seemed to have felt the same ambivalence about politics as Pak Sun-ch'on showed (see the section on the Virtuous Woman in this chapter). Her attitude toward her own legislative career may be described as that of a career woman toward her profession. She willingly accepted the challenging invitation to a political career and reached the pinnacle of her career at an early age. Her appointment to the national legislature meant to her a professional recognition of her ability as a political woman.

By the time her legislative appointment ended, however, she had witnessed various ugly scenes staged by her power-hungry colleagues that "sickened" her. Nonetheless, she acknowledges the presence of a small number of male colleagues with whom she shares the same values and admits that she would like to return to the political arena if they were given a chance to work as a team. Since she served in the legislature as a member of the ruling Democratic Republican Party during the Fourth Republic, however, it was difficult for her to reenter the political arena in the "new era" of the Fifth Republic under President Chun. She said during the interview that she spent her time mostly at home but continued to do part-time volunteer work for an association composed of former members of the defunct Democratic Republican Party. (She returned to active political life in 1988 by joining her former colleagues who formed the New Democratic Republican Party to participate in national politics of the Sixth Republic.)

The Heroic Woman

The fourth image of women legislators in Korea is the Heroic Woman, who pursues her goals in life single-mindedly. She refuses to be a traditional woman of virtue who sacrifices her life for the sake of her husband and children. Her life goal is to transcend the conventional gender boundaries and ascend to the highest level of human achievement. Gifted with "masculine" qualities (such as boldness and aggressiveness), she responds to the challenges of her time with a wholehearted dedication of her life.

The appearance and demeanor of a Heroic Woman fit the Korean concept of *yogol*. *Yogol* (literally, female hero) refers to a woman whose physical, psychological, and social characteristics are remarkably "unfeminine." The label *yogol* has both positive and negative connotations. It recognizes a woman's unusual, manly accomplishments, but at the same time stigmatizes her by pointing to her lack of femininity. Her physical features, such as height, weight, and strength, surpass those of an average woman and lend her an imposing appearance. Her personality traits include extraordinary bravery and integrity. In her social life she is a generous, charismatic leader.

Yim Yong-sin, who has been referred to as a *yogol* by various people, is a good example of the Heroic Woman. As described in Chapter 4, she married in her late thirties in the United States, but when her husband objected to her wholehearted involvement in the independence movement, she left him and returned to Korea to dedicate her life to national independence.

Yim Yong-sin played an important diplomatic role in the establishment of the Republic of Korea (see Chapter 5). She was the first female cabinet minister, the first woman lawmaker, the founder-president of Chungang University, the founder-president of the Korea Women's National Party. When she first ran for the vice-presidency in 1952, many people ridiculed her, and some called her a "crazy woman."[24] Yet with a strong determination and her lifelong credo, "To die for justice and to live for truth," she did what she believed was right.

When Yim Yong-sin announced her candidacy for the vice-presidency again in 1960, an editorial in *Dong-a Ilbo* (a major daily) called her a "skirted hero" (*ch'ima turun hogol*) and expressed a favorable interest in her leadership behavior.[25] When the election results revealed flagrant rigging (see Chapter 5), she boldly issued a denunciation of the fraudulent election. When the government of the Second Republic negotiated with Japan in what was perceived as an excessively conciliatory manner, Yim Yong-sin expressed her displeasure by issuing a critical statement in her capacity as president of the Korea Women's National Party.

In his eulogy for Yim Yong-sin, Yun Ch'i-yong (the first minister of home affairs and her longtime friend) quoted Song Chin-u (a respected patriot and politician) as having said that "*yogol* like Yim Yong-sin appears only once in four centuries."[26]

IN A MAN'S WORLD

Despite their very different leadership behaviors in political careers, both Yim Yong-sin, the vanguard Heroic Woman, and Pak Sun-ch'on, the neotraditional Virtuous Woman, faced the double bind and experienced the same inner conflict as women actively participating in the male-dominated political arena.

Yim Yong-sin possessed great self-confidence and assertiveness, which are necessary qualities for a successful politician. Yet, when these attributes are exhibited by a woman, they are regarded with discomfort and disapproval by most men. Yim's single status accorded her the freedom to devote herself to public life, but the lack of a respectable husband behind her often turned into a liability for her political efficacy in the Korean cultural context. According to Kim Ch'ol-an (who was one of Yim Yong-sin's protegees), Yim Yong-sin used to complain about her male colleagues looking down on her because of her marital status.

By contrast, Pak Sun-ch'on, who was the wife of a university president, tried not to forget good manners as a woman. A male informant who knew her well stated that she would restrain herself even when laughing with her male colleagues so that her laughter might not sound too loud and unfeminine. Her proper conduct and fulfillment of traditional feminine roles as mother and wife helped her earn the respect of her colleagues[27] and the position of leader in her party. Yet it was precisely because of her restrained womanly behavior—characteristic of a neotraditionalist woman—that Pak Sun-ch'on was unable to exercise her authority as a political party leader effectively.

Pak Sun-ch'on seemed to have experienced a great deal of internal conflict, since she did not approve the many ways her male colleagues conducted their political activities, yet could do very little to change them. Despite her illustrious career as a pioneer political woman, she seemed to have been greatly disillusioned at the end of her long political career. She wished that she had stayed in the field of social work rather than going into the male world of politics. Her ambivalent feelings toward her own political career may explain why she never groomed or encouraged other women to follow in her footsteps even though she acknowledged the need for more women in politics.

In this regard, it is interesting to note that even women politicians in the

United States today express the same internal conflict over their lives as political women, struggling to get into the political system while questioning it and wanting to change the way men operate it. Madeleine Kunin, governor of Vermont, stated that what is hard for any political woman is reconciling her internal self with the demands of the political system, "which is based on male traditions and is still largely male defined."[28] Kunin said that political women, who would like to change the rules of the game, find that if they do not play by the existing male-defined rules, they do not get to play at all.

Pak Sun-ch'on was able to play her role as a leading political woman by joining a major opposition party run by men and following their rules. In contrast, Yim Yong-sin led a women's political party, which she helped found after Liberation, and stayed with it until it was disbanded after the military revolution in 1961. Pak Sun-ch'on wrote that soon after Liberation when she invited Yim Yong-sin, who was busy forming a women's party, to join her in her women's association and suggested forming a political party later together with men, Yim Yong-sin refused by saying, "No way! I know what men are like."[29]

Yim Yong-sin became the first woman to be elected to the National Assembly. She also became the first woman candidate for vice-president and challenged for the same post twice without success. Had she joined a major political party, perhaps she may not have been nominated as a vice-presidential candidate. However, without belonging to a major party run by men and following their rules, she was unable to play a bigger role in politics.

The contrastive patterns and consequences of the behavioral responses that the two women legislators made to political life in Korea underscore the double bind in which women politicians across nations find themselves as a minority in the male-dominated world of politics.

NOTES

1. *Chubu Saenghwal,* May, 1985.

2. Kim and Pai (1981:92).

3. For various translations of *chiban,* see Brandt (1971:110), Cho (1979), and Choi (1984).

4. Murdock (1949).

5. Due to an illness she has suffered since 1982, Kim Ch'ol-an has lost weight. By the time of our interview in November, 1985, only her old photographs revealed how big she used to be.

6. Biernatzki (1967); Brandt (1971:108-21); Choi (1984); Janelli and Janelli (1982:135-44); T. Kim (1964); and M. Lee (1970).

7. Choi (1984).

8. Barringer (1980).

9. Kim and Pai (1981:73).

10. See Choi (1984) for a description of the various ways in which members of a clan demonstrated their social status and prestige to outsiders.

11. Son (1972:530).

12. Son (1972:535).

13. H. Kim (1975; 1977).

14. T. Yi (1986).

15. *Seoul Sinmun*, May 23, 1979.

16. In comparison, Ichikawa Fusae, her contemporary in Japanese politics, actively demonstrated the ways of "clean politics" in her own election campaigns (see Robins-Mowry 1983).

17. *Seoul Sinmun*, May 23, 1979.

18. T. Yi (1986:301).

19. The Democratic Party (Minjudang) and the Democratic Political Party (Minjongdang) combined their forces to create the Democratic People's Party (Minjungdang) in May, 1965.

20. *Seoul Sinmun*, May 23, 1979; T. Yi (1986).

21. In 1964, the unit of Korean currency, which was called *hwan*, was changed to *won*.

22. Rogers (1961:350).

23. Kanter (1977).

24. Son (1972:591).

25. *Dong-a Ilbo*, February 14, 1960, quoted in Son (1972:608).

26. See the foreword by Yun Ch'i-yong in Son (1972), as well as his eulogy for Yim in *Han'guk Ilbo*, February 20, 1977.

27. See, for example, the eulogy for Pak Sun-ch'on by Yu Ch'i-song (a male politician who had worked with her in the same opposition party) in *Dong-a Ilbo*, January 10, 1983.

28. Quoted in Goodman (1989).

29. Pak (1974-75:18).

9

Conclusion

The preceding chapters have amply shown the particularistic nature and limited scope of the participation of women in Korean politics. The analyses of the patterns of their career development have suggested at least three major variables for their attainment of high office in the National Assembly: personal backgrounds, political systems, and cultural-historical circumstances. This concluding chapter will first highlight some salient findings of this study in terms of both cultural particularities and general implications for women's representation in national politics. I will then briefly discuss the prospects and the recent development concerning women's participation in Korean politics.

The twenty-nine women legislators of this study were diverse in their occupational backgrounds, gender-role ideologies, motivations, and patterns of political participation. Nevertheless, we have found some striking commonalities in their social backgrounds, particularly in education and religion. The women legislators as a group were the educational elite of Korean society. The majority of women legislators of the pioneer generation received their formal education at girls' schools established by Christian missionaries in the early part of this century, when 90 percent of the female population were illiterate. Two pioneer women legislators studied further abroad, in Japan and in the United States. All the second-generation women legislators except one received higher education, and nearly half of the appointed women legislators had studied in the United States. Noteworthy also is the fact that more than half of the sample (seventeen) identified themselves as Christians, while only three identified themselves as Buddhists. When we remember that Buddhists greatly outnumbered Christians in Korea until recently,[1] the Christian predominance among women legislators is significant. Although we cannot measure the direct impact of high educational attainment and Christian faith on the development of legislative careers of these women, it is not hard to imagine how their education and religion must have positively contributed to a sense of competence and self-worth in them.

One could say that they were intellectually and psychologically prepared to take on new roles for women in a changing society.

The literature on women in politics has paid much attention to the importance of appropriate personality characteristics and untraditional socialization in producing political women.[2] The present study found a remarkable contrast in the socialization experiences of the elected versus appointed women legislators. The majority of elected women legislators had *absent fathers*, which meant that these women had been freed from strict patriarchal supervision and control in charting the course of their lives as political women.   In comparison, many appointed women legislators attributed their professional success to their *supportive fathers*, whose affectionate guidance laid the psychological groundwork for the daughters' entry into public life.

I have hypothesized elsewhere[3] that each of the two contrastive socialization patterns of the father-daughter relationship positively contributed to the daughter's acquisition of psychological androgyny and to her social achievement of professional success, through the psychosocial mechanism of liberation from traditional gender-role constraints and expectations. Androgyny, which may be defined as a balanced integration of positive "masculine" and "feminine" psychological characteristics, is regarded a requisite characteristic for effective leadership, according to recent research.[4] While there can be no denying the existence of some fundamental biological differences between the sexes, the findings of the present study suggest that traditional socialization practices, as important informal means of social control, contribute to the reproduction of many stereotyped behavioral differences between the sexes in social life. As long as politics continues to be male dominated, supportive fathers with an egalitarian worldview, I believe, will continue to be an important source of anticipatory socialization and the acquisition of psychological androgyny for professional women in leadership positions.

In terms of more directly identifiable motivations for political participation, the cases of all the elected women legislators of South Korea have indicated the paramount importance of deep *personal experience of politics* in producing political women. The overriding factor that motivated their political participation was a fervent sense of patriotic mission rather than a feminist awareness that "the personal is political."[5] In fact, their life histories suggest that "the political is personal," that is, that their pursuit of political careers was rooted in intense personal experiences of major political events. Their firsthand experiences of major political events (such as the March First Independence Movement, the postliberation political chaos, and the Korean War) deeply affected their political consciousness and generated strong personal desires to participate actively in national politics.[6] The degrees of their personal commitment to political life were indeed extraordinary. All the elected women legislators except one experienced incarceration for political reasons.

In contrast, an overwhelming majority of second-generation women became legislators owing to their accomplishments as successful professional women in such fields as college teaching, journalism, and women's organizations. However, because of the widespread negative perceptions of the proportional representation (PR) system itself among the general public (discussed in the foregoing chapters), and because the majority of women legislators owed their political careers to the PR system, there has been a tendency to categorically dismiss their contribution to the legislative process.[7] What should be pointed out here is that the many military generals who were appointed legislators were in fact as inexperienced as most women appointed legislators and that the National Assembly itself has not been able to function effectively in the politics of authoritarian regimes. Many appointed women legislators are self-actualized achievers of professional expertise and of leadership positions as the first females in various male-dominated, specialized fields. As such, their professional achievements have provided powerful testimonies to women's capabilities of working with their male counterparts as equal partners in the realization of a more just society. While the elected women legislators conjure up the images of courageous "fighters" (for national independence and for liberal democracy), many appointed women legislators should be recognized as quiet revolutionaries, spearheading gingerly the uncharted road of gender equality in the Korean patriarchal democracy.

The cross-national comparison of the ratio of women legislators in European countries, the United States, and Asian nations (as was presented in Chapter 6), has demonstrated the significance of electoral systems in affecting women's representation in political life. The experiences of women in Korean politics seemed to confirm the suggestion that electoral systems based on multiple-member constituencies and proportional representation party list systems led to higher representation of women in politics than did those based only on single-member constituencies.

The patterns of career development of Korean women legislators further suggested that periods of great political transition (e.g., from colonial rule to the establishment of a new nation, or from one republic to another) facilitated women's successful entry into the national legislature. Once the political transition took place and a new regime was established, however, the electoral system and the personal decisions of the top political leadership affected the extent of female representation in Korean politics.

Besides the electoral system, there are of course other situational variables such as the sociopolitical climate and patterns of political culture, which subtly but effectively hamper active participation of women in politics. We have noted that none of the women of this study became legislators by dint of being married to a politician husband, even though a "widow's succession" to the political post of a deceased husband has been a traditional means for women to enter politics in other cultures and nations. The lack of widow's succession in Korean political history is a cultural legacy that reflects the strength of the patrilineal social structure and the rigidity of the gender-role system in Korean society.[8] The low ratio of married women among my sample signified the difficulty of balancing marriage and career for professional women due to the rigid traditional division of labor in the patriarchal structure of the family. One might say that supportive husbands are essential ingredients for successful political careers of women. Not surprisingly, a great majority of the married appointed women legislators had a "love marriage," in which the husbands were supportive of their wives' professional careers, rather than the traditional arranged marriage. All the married elected women legislators except one also had very supportive husbands.

Even though women in modern Korea are now legally empowered to participate equally in public life, including politics, the organizational patterns of political culture (as shown in previous chapters) make it extremely difficult for women legislators to become equal partners with their male counterparts. The dominance of former military men in politics and the generally conservative attitude of the people toward women's roles in public life have unequivocally contributed to a climate particularly inimical to women's active participation in Korean politics.

Moreover, the contradictory, dualistic gender-role ideology of modern Korea has served as an invisible but powerful instrument to hamper the effectiveness of women legislators in their professional lives, thereby contributing to the status quo of the virtual male monopolization of formal political office. In the sociocultural context of the Korean patriarchal democracy, men and women tend to follow a compromise gender schema characterized by compartmentalization: That is, in order to handle the contradictions of dual gender-role ideologies, they compartmentalize the social arena (into public versus private spheres and formal and informal situations within each sphere) and alternate the guiding principle of gender relations in accordance with the situational variations and their good *nunch'i* (tact).

Under this paradigm of what I have called a "compartmentalized gender schema,"[9] a woman can claim her rightful place in politics and interact with men on an equal footing in public formal situations. In order to be an effective politician, however, a woman must use her *nunch'i* in the compartmentalized social arena and tread the fine line between the Confucian sensibility of proper behavior and the strong self-confidence and vision of a democratic leader. This seems to be a challenge that few women are willing to take. Some of the appointed women legislators in this study who are articulate and well qualified acknowledged the need for more women politicians but indicated that they themselves were unwilling to pursue a political career. They thought that to be a woman and a politician at the current stage of political development in South Korea was too tough a life and that it was not really worth the trouble.

In addition, many women—even of the younger generation—are still steeped in the patriarchal patterns of thoughts and beliefs. A recent study found, for instance, that 56.9 percent of Korean female college students believed in the male superiority in leadership behavior.[10] A plain fact is that the majority of Korean women voters would not support women candidates: A survey reported that 84 percent of women respondents thought male candidates were more capable as politicians than were female candidates, and 59 percent of women respondents stated that they would vote for a male candidate rather than a female candidate *even* when both were equally capable.[11] When Kim Ok-son (the only second-generation woman legislator elected three times) ran in the 1992 presidential election, nobody took her candidacy seriously; media coverage of her campaign was scant, and she lost. In the cultural context of South Korea, one can hardly imagine the kind of enthusiastic support that the people of the Philippines showed toward the candidacy of the "political widow" Corazon Aquino for president.[12]

Because of the precarious political situation of a divided nation-state, as well as the differentiated patterns of social change occurring in various sectors of modern Korea (urban versus rural areas, younger versus older generations, and blue-collar versus white-collar workers),[13] it is especially hazardous to predict the future of women's participation in national politics. Moreover, under the paradigm of a compartmentalized gender schema, the dividing line between the conservatives and the liberals in attitude toward gender role does not necessarily coincide with a social class distinction, nor does it reflect levels of education. Nonetheless, at this point the speculative question might be asked: What kind of women would be willing to commit themselves to the tough world of politics and become the third-generation political women of Korea?

A deep personal interest in politics by itself seems to be the most crucial motivational ingredient in the production of women politicians.[14] On the one hand, those young women who are actively involved in student or labor movements may accumulate enough deep personal experiences and interest to continue their political activism, but their radicalism may not be easily accepted by either the major political parties or the general public. On the other hand, female members of political parties constitute another pool of political women. A study of female partisans reported that 48.3 percent of female delegates to political parties aspired to run for legislative seats after acquiring sufficient political experience.[15] With the institutional resumption of the local legislatures in 1991, female political aspirants have new avenues for political careers open to them. A few women members of political parties and local legislatures may eventually be appointed to the National Assembly and/or be endorsed by their party to run for a national legislative seat.

So long as the present pattern of one-man rule continues to dominate the Korean political culture, however, much will depend on the top decision maker's beliefs and inclinations about women's role in political life. In this regard, the political career of Pak Yong-suk (whom I met and interviewed in 1990) is instructive. Pak, a longtime social activist, entered the political arena at the personal urgings of Kim Dae Jung, a major opposition leader, served as the vice-chair of the Peace and Democracy Party (P'yongmindang), and was appointed to the thirteenth National Assembly. As long as Kim Dae Jung was at the helm of the party, Pak enjoyed her leadership position within the party. However, after Kim Dae Jung formally declared his retirement from politics and left the party upon his defeat in the 1992 presidential election, Pak was unable to retain her leadership position. When the members of her party, now renamed the Democratic Party, elected eight executive members (Ch'oego Wiwon) during its 1993 national convention, Pak was not a winner. She finished tenth among eleven candidates.[16] This can be contrasted with her winning fourth place among the eight winners in the same kind of election held during the national convention in May, 1992, when Kim Dae Jung was nominated as the party's candidate for the presidency.[17] Without strong personal support from the top leader, Pak Yong-suk as the only woman candidate was unable to claim a leadership position in the male-dominated party.

It is the realities of the Korean political scene, such as the example sketched above, that incline me to remain rather pessimistic about the short-run prospects for women's *formal* representation in Korean politics under the current political culture and election system, despite the contrary opinion of a reviewer of the first edition of this book.[18] However, in tandem with the political reforms and liberalization trend since 1987 (see Chapter 1), grass-roots social and political activism among the citizenry of both sexes has notably increased in South Korea. Thus, it is outside the political structure that I have noted a very positive development in Korean women's political activism in the past few years, offering some basis for cautious optimism for long-term perspectives for women in Korean politics.

For instance, when I started the field research on women in Korean politics in 1985, there was only one women's organization (the Korean League of Women Voters) that was specifically concerned with women's participation in politics. By the summer of 1990, however, three women's organizations had been newly formed with the goal of improving women's roles and status in political life.[19] My interviews with the founders of these organizations revealed that two of them were political women who had competed in the 1989 general elections without success.[20] The third was a woman with a Ph.D. in political science. Together with the government-funded Korea Women's Development Institute, these private organizations have been actively engaged in raising women's political consciousness by conducting various seminars and sponsoring conferences on women and politics. They have also offered leadership-training workshops for female political aspirants, especially for the 1991 local elections. (Women won 0.9 percent of the seats in the local legislatures.[21]) The Korean League of Women Voters held a public forum to discuss with policy makers of major political parties their women-related platforms in the 1992 presidential election.[22] (President Kim Yong Sam fulfilled his election campaign promise by appointing three women to his cabinet in February, 1993.) The continued activism of these women's organizations will no doubt contribute to the politicization of women and to increasing women's representation in twenty-first-century Korean politics.

At the individual level, I believe a long-term strategy for enabling more women to gain access to national politics would be for women to penetrate the administrative and judiciary branches of the government. Since the higher civil servants in those branches are recruited by national examinations and a new regulation to eliminate sex distinction in the recruitment examination system for civil service was approved in June, 1989,[23] women will not suffer sexual discrimination at least in attaining their initial goals of entering civil service at the managerial level.

A record number of successful young women applicants in these examinations in 1985 indicates that women with higher educations have come to consider civil service as a career. Six young women (including a housewife) passed the national bar examination,[24] and three women in their early twenties were among the one hundred successful applicants for high-level civil service in 1985.[25] (By comparison, during the two decades after the establishment of the Republic of Korea, there were only two women who passed the bar examination, and the first time a woman passed the civil service examination was in 1973.) As was discussed in Chapter 6, the lack of civil service experience was one of the major differences in the occupational backgrounds of the male versus female appointed legislators of the twelfth National Assembly. By the time some of these young women entrants into civil service attain high positions in government, they will prove to be another pool of potential female candidates for the National Assembly.

However, so long as the patriarchal structure continues to dominate family life, preserving the traditonal patterns of gender-role division (which relegate child care and housekeeping to women), not many women will be able to afford the time and energy—let alone money—to pursue political careers.   A male appointed legislator who is a former professor of philosophy paid lip service to women's equal rights, but he emphasized that fulfillment of traditional feminine roles is too important for society and too time-consuming for the individual women for him to encourage women's active participation in national politics.

Also, without systemic support (such as a quota system guaranteeing a certain proportion of legislative seats to women), the near absence of women in the National Assembly will continue in the foreseeable future. The number of women legislators, in fact, steadily declined between 1981 and 1992 (see Tables 5.1 and 5.2). Although the proportional represenation (PR) system has been instrumental in the production of the overwhelming majority of Korean women legislators, its expedient use by the political leadership has kept women's representation through the PR system at a token level.   Among the four appointed women legislators of the fourteenth National Assembly, for example, only one could be regarded as representing women's interests, whereas the other three women were primarily representing their own professional fields (such as medicine/public health and fine/performing arts). As it is, politics is "a very harsh game" dominated by men, even in an advanced democracy like the United States.[26]

The rate of change in beliefs at the societal level is a very slow one. The Confucianization of Korean society, for example, took more than three centuries.[27] However, one may anticipate that transformations in values and life-styles will take place more quickly in the information age than in the premodern times. At any rate, a more equitable representation of the "fair" sex will occur only as a result of conscious social and political activism by women themselves to change the present androcentric social and political systems. Provided that women receive as much education as men and continue with their political struggle, Korean women should have achieved substantial progress toward a more egalitarian society by the centennial of the establishment of the Republic of Korea.

Nonetheless, barring some fundamental changes in the current social and political structure, the minority status of women's social and political positions will not improve without more women actively participating in the central institutions of the society.   Only when more women are personally committed to political life and earn the respect and empathy of their male counterparts will there be hope for a better representation of women in politics and for the elimination of social discrimination based on sex.   A nationally known former professor of history (who won a legislative seat in the 1992 general elections) believed that Korean men's "drawing room (*sarangbang*) politics" have failed to foster a democratic society and that Korean women should utilize their strength of character in national politics. What difference women politicians will make is an empirical question and secondary to the issue of gender equality. Elimination of social discrimination based on the sex or skin color of a person must be a major goal of all democratic societies.

NOTES

1. As of 1989, 19.7 percent of Koreans were Christians, slightly outnumbering Buddhists who made up 19 percent of the total population of more than 42 million in South Korea (see KOIS 1990:132-44). In comparison, in 1977, Buddhists constituted 35.4 percent of South Koreans, whereas Christians made up 16.7 percent of the total population of more than 36 million (see KOIS 1978:14, 205). For an encyclopedic synopsis of Christianity in Korea, see Soh (In press).

2. For a detailed discussion of socialization of women in politics, see Chou, Clark, and Clark (1990:121-138).

3. Soh (1993b).

4. See Cunn and Siegfried (1990).

5. For a discussion of the slogan, see Aerts (1986).

6. In this regard, it was interesting to observe how the 1991 Senate hearings on the confirmation of Judge Clarence Thomas to the U.S. Supreme Court (in which Professor Anita Hill testified against Judge Thomas, alleging his sexual harassment of her) seemed to have aroused the political consciousness of American women, especially about the total lack of women's representation among the fourteen members of the powerful Senate Judiciary Committee. Notably, many American women who ran in the 1992 congressional elections stated in various media coverages of their campaigns that the Senate hearings had *personally* motivated them to seek political office. A record number of women were elected to national office, making 1992 what many called the Year of the Woman. The percentage of women senators, for example, tripled (from 2 percent to 6 percent) after the 1992 elections.

7. The dismissal, one may add, is also a reflection of their relatively powerless positions among the political elite as a conspicuous but tiny minority. When I approached a leading publisher in Seoul about the possibility of having my work published by them, the editor-in-chief stated that nobody in Korea would be interested in reading a book about women legislators. The marginal status of women legislators as a tiny minority translated into an instant dismissal of even the utility of studying them.

8. One might state that there have been few "political families" to speak of in modern Korea owing to the colonial rule and the short history of the country as an independent nation-state. However, there have been at least a dozen recognizable political families in which sons and grandsons have succeeded to the political careers of their patrilineal ancestors (*Han'guk Ilbo*, April 15, 1991). In any case, it is almost impossible to imagine Korean politicians in the opposition camp asking the wife of Kim Dae Jung to run for the presidency, should the same tragedy have befallen him as the Philippine opposition leader Benigno Aquino.

9. For a detailed discussion of the paradigm, see Soh (1993a).

10. *Han'guk Ilbo* (Los Angeles edition), May 8, 1993.

11. *Kajong Sangdam*, August, 1989, p. 1.

12. As I indicated above in Note 8, the candidacy of a prominent "political widow" itself is unimaginable in Korean politics. For more details on a "Fairy-Tale Revolution" in the Philippines under the leadership of Corazon Aquino, see *Time*, January 5, 1987.

13. Barringer (1969); K. Kim (1985).

14. Clark and Clark (1986:15).

15. C. Yi (1985).

16. *Han'guk Ilbo* (Los Angeles edition), March 12, 1993.

17. *Han'guk Ilbo* (Los Angeles edition), May 27, 1992.

18. See Brandt (1993).

19. For more details, see *Chosun Ilbo*, June 14, 1990.

20. One of them, Kim Chong-suk, was appointed as the vice-minister to the Office of the Second Minister of State in 1993.

21. *Han'guk Ilbo* (Los Angeles edition), April 7, 1991.

22. *Han'guk Ilbo* (Los Angeles edition), March 8, 1992.

23. *Chungang Ilbo* (U.S. edition), June 10, 1989.

24. *Chosun Ilbo*, November 14, 1985.

25. *Chosun Ilbo*, December 3, 1985.

26. Jeane Kirkpatrick, quoted in *Time*, December 31, 1984.

27. Peterson (1983).

Appendix: Biographical Notes on Elected Women Legislators

KIM, CH'OL-AN (1912-92)

Born in Kimch'on as the first child of three girls. Took correspondence course from Meiji University in Japan. Taught at Kumnung Kindergarten in 1929. Participated in fund-raising activities for underground organizations for national independence during the Japanese colonial rule (1910-45). Married in 1934 and had four children.

Was deputy director of the Korea Young Women's Corps (Taehan Yoja Ch'ongnyondan) during the Korean War (1950-53). Was first elected to the National Assembly in 1954 and served for two consecutive terms (1954-60). Was elected to the chair of the Social and Health Committee in the third National Assembly in 1954.

KIM, CHONG-RYE (b. 1927)

Born in Tamyang as the last of eight children. Educated at the Special Training Class of Tamyang Girls' School in 1945. Received military training. Married in 1958 and has one son.

Joined the Liberal Party in 1951. Imprisoned for two years (1961-63) for an "antirevolution incident" after the 1961 military coup d'etat. Was banned from all political activities until 1968. Established the Korean League of Women Voters in 1969 and chaired it until 1981.

Was appointed to the Legislative Council for National Safeguarding (Kukka Powi Ippop Hoeui) in 1980. Joined the Democratic Justice Party in 1981. Served in the National Assembly for two terms from 1981 to 1988. Also served as the minister of health and social affairs from 1982 to 1985.

KIM, OK-SON (b. 1934)

Born in Changhang as the last of four children. Educated at Chongsin Girls' School in Seoul and at Chungang University, where she majored in political science. Has never married. Has always cross-dressed since she began her public life at the age of nineteen.

Was first elected to the seventh National Assembly (1967-71) as a member of the opposition party after winning a year-long legal battle against the fraudulent election of her opponent, who belonged to the ruling party. Was reelected to the ninth National Assembly (1973-79) but was compelled to resign because of the ire she caused President Park with her critical speech on dictatorship during a regular legislative session in 1975. Was sentenced to one year's imprisonment and two years' stay of execution for political reasons.

Was elected for the third time to the National Assembly in 1985 after ten years' forced absence from the political arena. On behalf of the opposition New Korea Democratic Party, presented "A Resolution for a Parliamentary Investigation to Verify the Kwangju Incident" to the Steering Committee of the twelfth National Assembly in 1985. Ran for the vice-chair of her party and for the vice-speaker of the National Assembly in 1985.

KIM, YUN-DOK (b. 1934)*

Born in Mokp'o as the sixth of twelve children. Educated at Mokp'o Girls' High School. After marriage in 1956, joined the Democratic Party in Mokp'o. Took up law at Song Kyun Kwan University in Seoul, graduating in 1964. Has six children.

Was director of the Women's Bureau of the New Democratic Party (Sinmindang). Served in the National Assembly for three terms (between 1971 and 1980) as a member of the opposition party. Was appointed president of the Korea Women's Development Institute in 1989.

*   (Kim Yun-dok informed me that the government record erroneously shows her birth year as being 1934. In fact, she was born in 1936.)

PAK, HYON-SUK (1896-1980)

Born in P'yongyang as the fourth of eight children. Educated at Sungui Girls' School in P'yongyang. Taught at Kijon Girls' School in Chonju and at her alma mater as well (1915-19). Married in 1919 and raised three children from her husband's first marriage. Had no child of her own.

Incarcerated three times—for over four years in total—for her anti-Japanese activities during the colonial rule (1910-45), including her active participation in the street demonstration march in P'yongyang during the March First Independence Movement of 1919.

Was appointed to the South Korean Interim Legislative Assembly in 1946 and to the Board of Inspection in 1948. Was a minister without portfolio in 1952. Was first elected to the National Assembly in 1958 and served her second term in the legislature as an appointed member (1963-67). Helped establish the President's Breakfast Prayer Association in the National Assembly in 1966. Was on the board of directors of Sungui Girls' High School in Seoul.

PAK, SUN-CH'ON (1898-1982)

Born in Tongnae as an only child. Given name was Myong-ryon. Adopted Sunch'on, her nickname of more than forty years, as her legal name in 1960. Got the alias Sunch'on-daek (a married woman from Sunch'on), in the days of her fugitive life after leading the street demonstration march in Masan during the March First Independence Movement of 1919. Served a year in prison for active participation in the national independence movement.

Was educated at Ilsin Girls' School in Pusan and at Nihon Women's University in Tokyo. Taught at Masan Girls' School (1917-19). Married in 1925 and had seven children. Was vice-principal of Chungang Girls' Middle School (1945) and a member of its board of directors (1972).

Was appointed to the Board of Inspection in 1948. Headed the Korea Women's Association (1951-54). Was first elected to the National Assembly in 1950 and served for five terms between 1950 and 1971. Was the leader of the main opposition party from 1963 to 1967.

YIM, YONG-SIN LOUISE (1899-1977)

Born in Kumsan as the fifth of twelve children of a local gentry family. Educated at Kijon Girls' School in Chonju and Hiroshima Christian College in Japan; received an M.A. in theology from the University of Southern California in 1931.

Taught at Yangdae Elementary School and Kongju High School. Was sentenced to a stay of execution for three and a half years for leading the street demonstration march in Chonju during the March First Independence Movement of 1919. Had a brief unsuccessful marital life in Los Angeles before returning to Korea by herself in 1940. Established Chungang University in Seoul.

Helped found the Korea Women's National Party in 1945 and headed it until 1961, when it was disbanded under the military rule. Acted as the delegate of the Representative Democratic Council of South Korea to the

United Nations to lobby for Korean independence (1946-48). Became first woman cabinet minister (1948) and first woman legislator (1949). Served in the National Assembly for two terms (1949-54). Ran for vice-president twice.

Glossary

Aeguk aejok. "Loving the nation and the people"; an idiom for patriotism.

Chagi. Oneself; used as a term of address among young people in contemporary South Korea.

Changmo. Mother-in-law.

Changnam. The first son.

Changnyo. The first daughter.

Chiban. The clan, the family, the household.

Ch'ima turun hogol. "A skirted hero" or *yogol*.

Chin'gol. "True-bone"; refers to the aristocracy of the lower rank in the *kolp'um* institution of the Silla dynasty (57 B.C.-935 A.D.).

Chong. Compassion.

Ch'onyo. An unmarried young woman; a virgin.

Ch'usok. A Korean day of Thanksgiving; the eighth full-moon day of the year.

Halmoni. Grandmother.

Hanbok. Traditional costume of the Koreans.

Hongilchom. "One red dot"; refers to the only female in the group.

Hubae. A junior graduate or member of an organization.

Hwan. The former unit of Korean currency (used until 1964).

Hwan'gap. The sixtieth birthday (marking a completion of the Chinese calendrical cycle).

Kojib. Stubbornness.

Kolp'um. "Bone rank"; refers to the status system of the royal clan in the Silla dynasty (57 B.C.-935 A.D.), which consisted of the *songgol* and *chin'gol* ranks.

Kosugi. A "hand-raising machine"; a pejorative term used in reference to appointed legislators, especially those of the ruling party during the Fourth Republic under President Park. They played an integral part in rubber-stamping government-proposed legislation.

Kuk. Nation; generally used in combination with another character (for example, *kukka*, the nation; *kukhoe*, the national assembly).

Kumbinyo. The ornamental gold rod used in the traditional hair style for married women.

K'unjol. A big bow; refers to a ritual performed to parents and/or ancestors by bending oneself in a semi-prostrate position and touching the floor with the hands placed against the forehead.

Kwigol. "Aristocratic bone"; refers to the facial bone structure of classic good looks suggesting a good family line (see *kolp'um*).

Mansokkun. A millionaire (in traditional Korea); used in reference to a wealthy owner of a huge farmland which yields an average of 10,000 *sok* of grain annually.

Mip'ung yangsok. Beautiful and good customs; often used in defense of traditional mores against Western influence.

Munjung. The lineage.

Namjang yogol. A *yogol* dressed in men's clothes.

Nim. A suffix attached to terms of address and reference expressing respect (for example, *changmo-nim* or *wonjang-nim*).

Nunch'i. Savoir faire or tact.

Nuna. An elder sister; used by male siblings.

Nunim. A respectful form of *nuna*.

Omoni. Mother.

P'adong. A crisis (of societal nature).

Poson. A stocking in the traditional Korean style.

Poson pallo. In stocking feet; in a great hurry.

Ppyodae innun chiban. A reputable family.

Sallim mitch'on. A household asset; used in reference to *changnyo*.

Samil Undong. March First Movement; refers to the grass-roots movement for national independence from Japanese rule which started on March 1, 1919.

Sarangbang. A drawing room; a living room reserved for the head of the family and his male guests in the traditional housing structure.

Soja. Illegitimate children.

Sok or *som.* A unit of measure of grain equal to 5.12 U.S. bushels.

Sonbae. A senior (relative to the *hubae*) graduate or member of an organization.

Sonbi. A scholar (in traditional Korea).

Songgol. "Sacred bone"; refers to the aristocracy of the higher rank in the *kolp'um* institution of Silla. Royal succession until Queen Chindok, the twenty-eighth monarch (r. 647-654), was limited to the *songgol* rank.

Songyok. A "sacred precinct"; refers to certain taboo subjects or areas of sociopolitical life for which freedom of speech is prohibited.

Sowon. A private academy where Chinese classics were taught in traditional Korea.

Ssugaech'ima. A veil; refers to a full-length shawl which women (until the early years of the twentieth century) wore over their heads to conceal their faces when going outside their homes.

Suryom ch'ongjong. "Administering state affairs from behind a curtain"; refers to regency by the queen mother in traditional Korea.

Uiwon. A representative.
Uri. We.

Won. The unit of Korean currency (since 1964); it replaced *hwan.*
Wonjang. The director or head of an organization.

Yangban. The civil official and the military official orders which controlled the affairs of government in the Koryo (918-1392) and the Yi (1392-1910) dynasties; refers to the ruling or upper class in traditional Korea.
Yogol. An extraordinary woman of "manly" qualities.

References

Adler, Alfred. 1924. *The Practice and Theory of Individual Psychology*. P. Radin, trans. New York: Harcourt, Brace. (Originally published in 1920.)

————. 1964. *Problems of Neurosis*. New York: Harper and Row. (Originally published in 1930.)

Aerts, Mieke. 1986. Catholic Constructions of Femininity: Three Dutch Women's Organizations in Search of a Politics of the Personal, 1912-1940. In *Women in Culture and Politics: A Century of Change*. J. Friedlander et al., eds. Bloomington: Indiana University Press.

Apter, David E. 1981. Korea in Perspective—Some Thoughts on Economic Success and Political Failure. In *Modernization of Korea and the Impact of the West*. C. Lee, ed. Los Angeles: University of Southern California.

Barringer, Herbert R. 1969. Social Change and Social Differentiation in Korea. In *Aspects of Social Change in Korea*. E. Kim and C. Chee, eds. Michigan: Korea Research and Publications.

————. 1980. Social Differentiation, Stratification and Mobility. In *Korea: A Decade of Development*. Y. Chang, ed. Seoul: Seoul National University Press.

Bean, Susan S. 1989. Gandhi and *Khadi*: The Fabric of Indian Independence. In *Cloth and Human Experience*. A. B. Weiner and J. Schneider, eds. Washington: Smithsonian Institution Press.

Bennett, Linda. 1986. Meet the Other Women Heads of Nations. *Ms.* 15(4):86.

Biernatzki, William E. 1967. Varieties of Korean Lineage Structure. Ph.D. dissertation, St. Louis University.

Bodde, Derk. 1953. Harmony and Conflict in Chinese Philosophy. In *Studies in Chinese Thought*. Arthur F. Wright, ed. Chicago: University of Chicago Press.

Brandt, Vincent S. R. 1971. *A Korean Village: Between Farm and Sea*. Cambridge, Mass.: Harvard University Press.

————. 1993. [Review of *The Chosen Women in Korean Politics: An Anthropological Study*]. *Korea Journal* 33(1):107-109.

Burton, Roger V., and John W. M. Whiting. 1961. The Absent Father and Cross-Sex Identity. *Merrill-Palmer Quarterly* 7(2):85-96.

Central Commission for Election Management (CCEM). N.d. *Che 13-dae kukhoe uiwon son'go ch'ongnam (1988.4.26 sihaeng)*. Seoul: Chungang Son'go Kwalli Wiwonhoe.

Cha, Jae-ho, Bom-mo Chung, and Sung-jin Lee. 1977. Boy Preference Reflected in Korean Folklore. In *Virtues in Conflict: Tradition and the Korean Woman Today*. S. Matielli, ed. Seoul: Samhwa Publishing.

Cheon, Kum Sung. 1982. *Chun Doo Hwan: Man of Destiny: A Biography of the President of the Republic of Korea*. W. Y. Joh, trans. Los Angeles: North American Press.

Cho, Oak-la. 1979. Social Stratification in a Korean Peasant Village. Ph.D. dissertation, State University of New York, Stony Brook.

Chodorow, Nancy. 1974. Family Structure and Feminine Personality. In *Woman, Culture, and Society*. M. Z. Rosaldo and L. Lamphere, eds. Stanford: Stanford University Press.

Ch'oe, Pong-dae. 1985. Chongch'ijok ideologi rul t'onghae bon Yi Sungman chongkwon ui songnip kwajong gwa ku hamui. In *Han'guk hyondaesa I*. Chang-jip Ch'oe, ed. Seoul: Yorumsa.

Ch'oe, Tae-ung. 1972. Kodokhan soninjang. In *Changmi eso komok uro: So t'aehu; Minbi; Pak Sun-ch'on*. Seoul: Samjinsa.

Choi, Jai-seuk. 1984. Lineage Organization and Its Functions in Korea: A Case Study of Hadong Chong-ssi. *Journal of Social Sciences and Humanities* 59:103-14.

Chou, Bih-er, and Janet Clark. 1986. Women Legislators in Taiwan: Barriers to Women's Political Participation in a Modernizing State. Office of Women in International Development, Working Paper no. 119. East Lansing: Michigan State University.

Chou, Bih-er, Cal Clark, and Janet Clark. 1990. *Women in Taiwan Politics: Overcoming Barriers to Women's Participation in a Modernizing Society*. Boulder & London: Lynne Rienner.

Chung, Chai-sik. 1982. Confucian Tradition and Values: Implications for Conflict in Modern Korea. In *Religions in Korea: Beliefs and Cultural Values*. E. H. Phillips and E. Y. Yu, eds. Los Angeles: California State University Press.

Chung, David. 1961. A Narrative of Christianity in Social Change of Korea since the Seventeenth Century. *Journal of Social Sciences and Humanities* 14:1-32.

Clark, C., and J. Clark. 1986. Models of Gender and Political Participation in the United States. *Women & Politics* 6(1):5-25.

Clark, Donald N. 1986. *Christianity in Modern Korea*. Lanham, Md.: University Press of America.

————, ed. 1988. *The Kwangju Uprising: Shadows over the Regime in*

South Korea. Boulder, Colo.: Westview Press.
————. 1991. Bitter Friendship: Understanding Anti-Americanism in South Korea. In *Korea Briefing, 1991.* D. Clark, ed. Boulder, Colo.: Westview Press.
Clifford, James. 1978. "Hanging Up Looking Glasses at Odd Corners": Ethnobiographical Prospects. In *Studies in Biography.* D. Aaron, ed. Cambridge, Mass.: Harvard University Press.
Crandall, Virginia C., and Beth W. Crandall. 1983. Maternal and Childhood Behaviors as Antecedents of Internal-External Control Perceptions in Young Adulthood. In *Research with the Locus of Control Construct,* vol. 2. H. M. Lefcourt, ed. New York: Academic Press.
Cumings, Bruce. 1984. *The Two Koreas.* New York: Foreign Policy Association.
Cunn, Arnie, and William D. Siegfried. 1990. Gender Stereotypes and Dimensions of Effective Leader Behavior. *Sex Roles* 23:413-19.
D'Andrade, Roy G. 1973. Father Absence, Identification, and Identity. *Ethos* 1(4):440-55.
Darcy, R., and Sunhee Song. 1986. Men and Women in the South Korean National Assembly: Social Barriers to Representational Roles. *Asian Survey* 26(6):670-87.
De Vos, George, and Kwang-kyu Lee. 1981. An Inquiry about Possible Dilemmas of Authority in Post Colonial Korean Modernization. In *Modernization of Korea and the Impact of the West.* C. Lee, ed. Los Angeles: University of Southern California.
Dhawan, S. K. 1985. *Selected Thoughts of Indira Gandhi: A Book of Quotes.* Delhi: Mittal Publications.
Dix, Griffin M. 1980. The Place of the Almanac in Korean Folk Religion. *Journal of Korean Studies* 2:47-70.
Dong-a Yon'gam. 1985. Seoul: Dong-a Ilbosa.
Eckert, Carter, Ki-back Lee, Young Ick Lew, Michael Robinson, and Edward W. Wagner. 1990. *Korea Old and New: A History.* Seoul: Ilchokak.
Firth, Raymond. 1954. Social Organization and Social Change. *Journal of the Royal Anthropological Institute* 84:1-20.
Forer, Lucille K. 1977. Bibliography of Birth Order Literature in the '70's. *Journal of Individual Psychology* 33(1):122-41.
Goodman, Ellen. 1989. Politics: It's still a man's world. *The Honolulu Advertiser,* October 20.
Gosfield, F., and B. J. Hurwood. 1969. *Korea: Land of the 38th Parallel.* New York: Parents' Magazine Press.
Ha, Tae-hung. 1958. *Folk Customs and Family Life.* Seoul: Yonsei University Press.
Hahm, Pyong-choon. 1975. Toward a New Theory of Korean Politics: A

Reexamination of Traditional Factors. In *Korean Politics in Transition*. E. R. Wright, ed. Seattle and London: University of Washington Press.

Han, Pae-ho. 1984. *Han'guk ui chongch'i*. Seoul: Pakyongsa.

Han, Sungjoo. 1974. *The Failure of Democracy in South Korea*. Berkeley: University of California Press.

Han'guk Gallup Chosa Yon'guso. 1984. *Yosong chongch'iga e taehan chon kungmin ui yoron*. Seoul: Han'guk Gallup Chosa Yon'guso.

Harvey, Youngsook Kim. 1979. *Six Korean Women: The Socialization of Shamans*. St. Paul, Minn.: West Publishing.

Henderson, Gregory. 1968. *Korea: The Politics of the Vortex*. Cambridge, Mass.: Harvard University Press.

Hennig, Margaret, and Anne Jardim. 1977. *The Managerial Woman*. New York: Pocket Books.

Hoffer, Carol P. 1972. Mende and Sherbro Women in High Office. *Canadian Journal of African Studies* 6(2):151-64.

Jacobs, Norman. 1985. *The Korean Road to Modernization and Development*. Urbana: University of Illinois Press.

Janelli, Roger L., and Dawnhee Y. Janelli. 1982. *Ancestor Worship and Korean Society*. Stanford: Stanford University Press.

Jayawardena, Kumari. 1986. *Feminism and Nationalism in the Third World*. London: Zed Books.

Jones, H. J. 1975. Japanese Women in the Politics of the Seventies. *Asian Survey* 15(8):708-23.

Kammeyer, Kenneth. 1966. Birth Order and the Feminine Sex Role among College Women. *American Sociological Review* 31(4):508-15.

Kang, Jangseok. 1988. Conflict Management in Divisive Legislatures: A Theory and Application to Korean Legislative Conflicts. Ph.D. dissertation, University of Hawaii at Manoa.

Kang, Wi Jo. 1986. Relations between the Japanese Colonial Government and the American Missionary Community in Korea, 1905-1945. In *One Hundred Years of Korean-American Relations, 1882-1982*. Yur-Bok Lee and Wayne Patterson, eds. University, Al.: University of Alabama Press.

————. 1987. *Religion and Politics under the Japanese Rule*. Lewiston: Edwin Mellen Press.

Kanter, Rosabeth M. 1977. *Men and Women of the Corporation*. New York: Basic Books.

Kelly, R. M., and M. Boutilier. 1978. *The Making of Political Women: A Study of Socialization and Role Conflict*. Chicago: Nelson-Hall.

Kendall, Laurel. 1988. *The Life and Hard Times of a Korean Shaman: Of Tales and the Telling of Tales*. Honolulu: University of Hawaii Press.

Kim, Chong-lim, and Seong-tong Pai. 1981. *Legislative Process in Korea*. Seoul: Seoul National University Press.

Kim, Haingja. 1975. A Comparative Study of the U.S. House of

Representatives and the National Assembly of Korea: A Cross-Cultural Study Focusing on Role Analysis of Female Politicians.   Ph.D. dissertation, University of Hawaii at Manoa.

—————. 1977.   Role Analysis of Female Politicians in Korea: A Comparison with U.S. Congresswomen. *Korea Journal* 17(7):35-43.

Kim, Hak-chun . 1983. *Han'guk chongch'iron: Yon'gu ui hyonhwang kwa panghyang.* Seoul: Han'gilsa.

Kim, Helen Hwal-lan. 1965. *Ku pitsok ui chakun saengmyong.* Seoul: Yowonsa.

Kim, Ki-bom. 1974a. Revisions of the Korean Constitution (I). *Korea Journal* 14(7):4-13.

—————. 1974b. Revisions of the Korean Constitution (II). *Korea Journal* 14(8):18-25.

Kim, Kyong-dong. 1985. Social Change and Societal Development in Korea since 1945. *Korea and World Affairs* 9(4):756-88.

Kim, Kyo-sik. 1984. Han'guk ch'oech'o ui yosong chongch'iin Pak Sun-ch'on. *Chubu Saenghwal,* January, 120-52.

Kim, Ok-son. 1984. Nuga nae otsul potkyotnunya. *Chubu Saenghwal,* September, 103-10.

—————. 1985. *Kukhoe puuichang sonch'ul e chuumhayo.* Press release dated August 23.

Kim, Pu-sik, et al. 1983 Samguk sagi. Translated and annotated by Pyong-do Yi. Seoul: Ulyu. (Originally compiled in 1145.)

Kim, Se-Jin, and Chang-Hyun Cho, eds. 1972. *Government and Politics of Korea.* Silver Springs, Md.: Research Institute on Korean Affairs.

Kim, T'aek-kyu. 1964. *Tongjok purak ui saenghwal kujo yon'gu.* Taegu: Ch'onggu University Press.

Kim, Yung-Chung, ed. and trans. 1979. *Women of Korea: A History from Ancient Times to 1945.* Seoul: Ewha Womans University Press.

Kirkpatrick, Jeane J. 1974. *Political Woman.* New York: Basic Books.

Kluckhohn, Clyde. 1945. The Personal Document in Anthropological Science. In *The Use of Personal Documents in History, Anthropology, and Sociology.* L. Gottschalk, C. Kluckhohn, and R. Angell. New York: Social Science Research Council.

Koh, Hesung Chun. 1975. Yi Dynasty Korean Women in the Public Domain: A New Perspective on Social Stratification. *Social Science Journal* 13:7-19.

Korea Overseas Information Service (KOIS). 1978. *A Handbook of Korea.* Second ed. Seoul: KOIS.

—————. 1980. *Constitution: Korea Background Series,* vol. 1. Seoul: KOIS.

—————. 1987. *A Handbook of Korea.* Sixth ed. Seoul: KOIS.

—————. 1990. *A Handbook of Korea.* Eighth ed. Seoul: KOIS.

Korea Women's Association (KWA). 1986. *Han'guk yosung undong yaksa.*

Seoul: Han'guk puinhoe ch'ongbonbu.

Korea Women's Development Institute (KWDI). 1985. *Yosong paekso*. Seoul: Han'guk yosong kaebalwon.

————. 1991. *Yosong paekso*. Seoul: Han'guk yosong kaebalwon.

Kusano, Jun. 1985. *Chotto Shiritai Kankoku*. Tokyo: Sanshuusha.

Leach, Edmond. 1954. *Political Systems of Highland Burma*. London: Athlone Press.

Lebra, Takie Sugiyama. 1981. Japanese Women in Male Dominant Careers: Cultural Barriers and Accommodations for Sex-Role Transcendence. *Ethnology* 20(4):291-306.

Lee, Changsoo. 1981. Civil-Military Relations and the Emergence of "Civilitary" Bureaucrats in Korea. In *Modernization of Korea and the Impact of the West*. C. Lee, ed. Los Angeles: University of Southern California.

Lee, Hyo-chae. 1977. Protestant Missionary Work and Enlightenment of Korean Women. *Korea Journal* 17(11):33-50.

————. 1980. Women as Victims of the Dual Marriage System in Korea. *Journal of Social Sciences and Humanities* 51:1-8.

————. 1985. *Pundansidae ui sahoehak*. Seoul: Han'gilsa.

Lee, Hyo-chae, and Chu-suk Kim. 1976. *Han'guk yosong ui chiwi*. Seoul: Ewha yoja taehakkyo ch'ulp'anbu.

————. 1977. The Status of Korean Women Today. In *Virtues in Conflict: Tradition and the Korean Woman Today*. S. Mattielli, ed. Seoul: Samhwa Publishing.

Lee, Ki-baik. 1984. *A New History of Korea*. Edward W. Wagner with Edward J. Shultz, trans. Seoul: Ilchogak.

Lee, Mangap. 1970. Consanguineous Group and Its Function in the Korean Community. In *Families in East and West*. R. Hill and R. Konig, eds. The Hague: Mouton.

Levi-Strauss, Claude. 1969. *The Elementary Structures of Kinship*. J. H. Bell and J. R. von Sturmer, trans., and Rodney Needham, ed. Boston: Beacon Press.

Lovell, John P. 1975. The Military and Politics in Postwar Korea. In *Korean Politics in Transition*. E. R. Wright, ed. Seattle: University of Washington Press.

Lynn, Naomi B. 1979. American Women and the Political Process. In *Women: A Feminist Perspective*. Jo Freeman, ed. Palo Alto, Calif.: Mayfield Publishing.

McBrian, Charles D. 1977. Two Models of Social Structure and Manifest Personality in Korean Society. In *Occasional Papers on Korea* 5:1-7. Seattle: University of Washington.

McCann, David R. 1983. Formal and Informal Korean Society: A Reading of Kisaeng Songs. In *Korean Women: View from the Inner Room*.

L. Kendall and M. Peterson, eds. New Haven: East Rock Press.

McCune, George M. 1950. Korea Today. Cambridge, Mass.: Harvard University Press.

Mandelbaum, David. 1973. The Study of Life History: Gandhi. *Current Anthropology* 14(3):177-96.

Means, Ingunn N. 1972. Women in Local Politics: The Norwegian Experience. *Canadian Journal of Political Science* 5(3):365-88.

Merton, Robert K. 1957. *Social Theory and Social Structure*. New York: Free Press.

Michael, Prince of Greece. 1986. I Am Fantastically Lucky. *Parade*, July 13, 4-7.

Miley, C. H. 1969. Birth Order Research 1963-1967: Bibliography and Index. *Journal of Individual Psychology* 25:64-70.

Murdock, George P. 1949. *Social Structure*. New York: Free Press.

Nakayama, Kazuyoshi. 1985. Introduction. In *Fukuzawa Yukichi on Education: Selected Works*. Eiichi Kiyooka, trans. and ed. Tokyo: University of Tokyo Press.

National Assembly of the Republic of Korea (NA). 1985. *Kukhoe Such'op 1985*. Seoul: Taehan Min'guk Kukhoe.

National History Compilation Committee (NHCC). 1968. *Charyo Taehan Min'guksa*. vol. 1-7. Seoul: Kuksa P'yonch'an Wiwonhoe.

Newland, Kathleen. 1975. *Women in Politics: A Global Review*. Worldwatch Paper 3. Washington, D.C.: Worldwatch Institute.

Office of the Second Minister of State (OSMS). 1990. *Kajokpop ottotk'ke pakkwionna*. Seoul:Chongmujangkwan che 2 sil.

Oh, Bonnie B. 1982. From Three Obediences to Patriotism and Nationalism: Women's Status in Korea up to 1945. *Korea Journal* 22(7):37-55.

Oh, Byung-hun. 1975. Students and Politics. In *Korean Politics in Transition*. E. R. Wright, ed. Seattle: University of Washington Press.

Oliver, Robert T. 1954. *Syngman Rhee: The Man Behind the Myth*. New York: Dodd Mead.

————. 1978. *Syngman Rhee and American Involvement in Korea, 1942-1960: A Personal Narrative*. Seoul: Panmun Book.

Om, Kwang-yong. 1986 Kim Ok-son: Kangkyong palon uro uiwonjik sat'oehan yosong uiwon. *Kajong Chosun*, January, 306-8.

Ortner, Sherry B. 1974. Is Female to Male as Nature Is to Culture? In *Woman, Culture, and Society*. M. Z. Rosaldo and L. Lamphere, eds. Stanford: Stanford University Press.

Osgood, Cornelius. 1951. *The Koreans and Their Culture*. New York: Ronald Press.

Pahk, Induk. 1954. *September Monkey*. New York: Harper and Brothers.

Pak, Sun-ch'on. 1968. Pak Sun-ch'on chasojon: Ulmit e son pongsonhwa ya. *Yowon*, May.

―――――. 1974-75. Na-ui iryokso. *Han'guk Ilbo*, November 16, 1974-January 8, 1975. Seoul: Han'guk Ilbosa.

Palais, James B. 1975. *Politics and Policy in Traditional Korea*. Cambridge, Mass.: Harvard University Press.

Pang, Ki-hwan. 1980. *Yosong han'guksa*. Seoul: Seilsa.

Park, Chung Hee. 1979. *Korea Reborn: A Model for Development*. Englewood Cliffs, N.J.: Prentice-Hall.

Parker, Seymour, Janet Smith, and Joseph Ginat. 1975. Father Absence and Cross-Sex Identity: The Puberty Rites Controversy Revisited. *American Ethnologist* 2:687-706.

Peterson, Mark. 1983. Women without Sons: A Measure of Social Change in Yi Dynasty Korea. In *Korean Women: View from the Inner Room*. L. Kendall and M. Peterson, eds. New Haven, Conn.: East Rock Press.

Pharr, Susan J. 1977. Japan: Historical and Contemporary Perspectives. In *Women: Roles and Status in Eight Countries*. J. Z. Giele and A. C. Smock, eds. New York: Wiley.

―――――. 1981. *Political Women in Japan: The Search for a Place in Political Life*. Berkeley: University of California Press.

Promotion Committee to Commemorate the Sixtieth Birthday of Dr. Yim Yong-sin (PCC). 1959. *Yim Yong-sin Paksa: Pitnanun saengae*. Seoul: Yim Yong-sin Paksa Hoegap Kinyom Saop Ch'ujin Wiwonhoe.

Pye, Lucian. 1985. *Asian Power and Politics: The Cultural Dimensions of Authority*. Cambridge, Mass.: Harvard University Press.

Quinn, Naomi. 1977. Anthropological Studies on Women's Status. *Annual Review of Anthropology* 6:181-225.

Radcliffe-Brown, Alfred R. 1940. On Social Structure. *Journal of the Royal Anthropological Institute* 70:1-12.

Randall, Vicky. 1987. *Women and Politics: An International Perspective*. Second ed. Chicago: University of Chicago Press.

Robins-Mowry, Dorothy. 1983. *The Hidden Sun: Women of Modern Japan*. Boulder, Colo.: Westview Press.

Rogers, Carl R. 1961. *On Becoming a Person*. Boston: Houghton Mifflin.

Rosaldo, Michelle Z. 1974. Woman, Culture, and Society: A Theoretical Overview. In *Woman, Culture, and Society*. M. Z. Rosaldo and L. Lamphere, eds. Stanford: Stanford University Press.

Rossi, Alice. 1965. Naming Children in Middle-Class Families. *American Sociological Review* 30(4):499-513.

Santrock, John W., and Richard A. Warshak. 1979. Father Custody and Social Development in Boys and Girls. In *Journal of Social Issues* 35(4):112-25.

Scalapino, Robert A. 1981. Korean Politics―Tradition and Change in an

Era of Crisis. In *Modernization of Korea and the Impact of the West*. C. Lee, ed. Los Angeles: East Asian Studies Center, University of Southern California.

Schlegel, Alice. 1977. Toward a Theory of Sexual Stratification. In *Sexual Stratification: A Cross-Cultural View*. A. Schlegel, ed. New York: Columbia University Press.

Scott, Joan W. 1986. Gender: A Useful Category of Historical Analysis. *American Historical Review* 91:1053-75.

Seneviratne, Maureen. 1975. *Sirimavo Bandaranaike: The World's First Woman Prime Minister*. Colombo: Hansa.

Sheridan, Mary, and Janet W. Salaff, eds. 1984. *Lives: Chinese Working Women*. Bloomington: Indiana University Press.

Shulman, Bernard H., and Harold H. Mosak. 1977. Birth Order and Ordinal Position: Two Adlerian Views. *Journal of Individual Psychology* 33:114-21.

Silver, Catherine B. 1973. Salon, Foyer, Bureau: Women and the Professions in France. In *Changing Women in a Changing Society*. J. Huber, ed. Chicago: University of Chicago Press.

Sivard, Ruth Leger. 1985. Women: A World Survey. Washington, D.C.: World Priorities.

Smolowe, Jill. 1989. A Mountain Moves. *Time* 134 (6):24-26.

So, Ik-won. 1984. Che 3 konghwaguk pihwa palgul. *Chugan Han'guk*, October 27.

Soh, Chung Hee. 1988. Korean Women in Politics (1945-1985): A Study of the Dynamics of Gender Role Change (Ph.D. dissertation, University of Hawaii at Manoa, 1987). *Dissertation Abstracts International* 48, 1817A-1818A. (University Microfilms No. 8722393)

————. 1991. *The Chosen Women in Korean Politics: An Anthropological Study*. New York: Praeger.

————. 1992. Skirts, Trousers, or *Hanbok*?: The Politics of Image Making among Korean Women Legislators. *Women's Studies International Forum* 15:375-384.

————. 1993a. Sexual Equality, Male Superiority, and Korean Women in Politics: Changing Gender Relations in a "Patriarchal Democracy." *Sex Roles* 28:73-90.

————. 1993b. Fathers and Daughters: Paternal Influence among Korean Women in Politics. *Ethos* 21:53-78.

————. In press. Christianity in Korea. In *The Asian American Encyclopedia*. North Bellmore, NY: Marshall Cavendish.

Son, Ch'ung-mu. 1972. *Han'gang-un hurunda*. Seoul: Dong-a Ch'ulp'ansa.

Stone, Gregory. 1965. Appearance and the Self. In *Dress, Adornment, and the Social Order*. M. E. Roach and J. B. Eicher, eds. New York: Wiley.

Strawn, Sonia R. 1981. Dr. Lee Tae-Young and the Korean Family Law.

Transactions of the Royal Asiatic Society, Korea Branch 56:37-45.

Sungui Publication Committee (SPC). 1968. *Simundaero.* Seoul: Sungui Ch'ulp'an Wiwonhoe.

Thornton, Arland, Alwin F. Duane, and Donald Camburn. 1983. Causes and Consequences of Sex-Role Attitudes and Attitude Change. *American Sociological Review* 48:211-27.

Tieszen, Helen Rose. 1977. Korean Proverbs about Women. In *Virtues in Conflict.* S. Mattielli, ed. Seoul: Samhwa Publishing.

Turner, Victor. 1969. *The Ritual Process: Structure and Anti-Structure.* Ithaca: Cornell University Press.

Vallance, Elizabeth. 1979. *Women in the House: A Study of Women Members of Parliament.* London: Athlone Press.

Vockell, E. L., D. W. Felker, and C. H. Miley. 1973. Birth Order Literature 1967-1971: Bibliography and Index. *Journal of Individual Psychology* 29:39-53.

Werner, Emmy E. 1966. Women in Congress: 1917-1964. *Western Political Quarterly* 19(1):16-30.

Wright, Edward R., ed. 1975. *Korean Politics in Transition.* Seattle: University of Washington Press.

Yi, Ch'un-ho. 1985. Yosong ui chongch'i ch'amyo e kwanhan yon'gu. M.A. thesis, Ewha Women's University.

Yi, Hye-song. 1984. Yoja kyosu ui songch'ui tonggi e kwanhan saryeyon'gu. *Yosonghak nonjip* 1:24-55.

Yi, Hyon-hi. 1982. *Han'guk kundae yosong kaehwasa.* Seoul: Yiwu.

Yi, Man-yol, ed. 1985. *Han'guksa yonp'yo.* Seoul: Yokminsa.

Yi, To-hi. 1986. Pak Sun-ch'on: Chongch'i e kanghago chong e yakhaetton ch'oech'o ui yodangsu. *Kajong Chosun,* January.

Yim, Chung-bin. 1985. Pak Sun-ch'on halmoni wa Yuk Yong-su yosa. *Yosong Dong-a,* July, 82-91.

Yim, Louise. 1951. *My Forty Year Fight for Korea.* Seoul: Chungang University.

Yun, Chae-hyong. 1985. Kim Ok-son uiwon. *Yosong Chasin,* September.

Yun, Ch'on-ju. 1979. *Han'guk chongch'i ch'egye.* Seoul: Seoul Taehakkyo Ch'ulp'anbu.

KOREAN NEWSPAPERS AND PERIODICALS

Chosun Ilbo	Kajong Chosun	Sina Ilbo
Chubu Saenghwal	Kajong Sangdam	Taehan Ilbo
Chugan Han'guk	Korea Times	Yosong Chasin
Chungang Ilbo	Kyonghyang Sinmun	Yosong Dong-a
Dong-a Ilbo	Maeil Sinbo	Yowon
Han'guk Ilbo	Seoul Sinmun	

About the Book and Author

Chunghee Sarah Soh here contributes a unique perspective on women in politics by examining the experiences of Korean women in their national legislature. The major questions she raises are: Who are these women? How did they attain their political positions? What motivated their participation in male-dominated politics? What insights would an analysis of their personal and professional experiences provide to our understanding of complex processes of social change? How do the experiences of women in Korean politics compare with those of their counterparts in different nation-states?

By analyzing the life histories of twenty-nine women legislators in the South Korean National Assembly, Professor Soh illuminates many aspects of modern Korean society, as well as the dynamics of changing male-female relations and gender-role conceptions in a modernizing society. The author adds an important new dimension to the study of women in politics by situating her findings in the broader sociohistorical context of a "patriarchal democracy." Soh also provides cross-cultural comparative perspectives on such topics as family backgrounds, gender-role socialization, patterns of recruitment, and the impact of the electoral system on the representation of women in national politics.

In this new edition, the introductory and concluding chapters have been rewritten, and relevant parts in the text have been updated to reflect the fast pace of social change in South Korea.

Chunghee Sarah Soh is assistant professor of anthropology at Southwest Texas State University. She received her Ph.D. from the University of Hawaii, where she was an East-West Center grantee. Her research on Korean women in politics was funded by grants from the National Science Foundation and the East-West Center. She taught at universities in Korea and Hawaii. She was a visiting assistant professor of anthropology at the University of Arizona, 1990-91.

Index

absent father: effect on daughter's development, 27, 132; prevalence of, among pioneer generation of women legislators, 26. *See also* father

absolute obedience, 110

Acheson, Dean, 96

active participation in public life, women's, 59-60; criticism of, 55, 104; effect on gender-role attitude, 50; traditional Korea, 17-20; variables for, 131

activism. *See* grass-roots activism; women's activism

adaptationist attitude, 115, 117 (*see also* gender-role change, dynamics of); examples of, 116

administrative and managerial positions, women in, 2

adoption practices, 16

affinal parents, 114

aides, 96-98; male vs. female, 97-98

alias, 36

Andong, 60, 78, 102

androgyny: defined, 132. *See also* socialization

Anti-American sentiment, 9, 14 n.28

anticipatory socialization, 28, 132. *See also* socialization; supportive father

appearance: conspicuous, 104; gender-specific, 105; manly, 103-4; sensitivity to, 105. *See also* dress styles

appointed legislators: categories of, 89-90; definition of, 8; education, 33, 38-39; female vs. male, 39, 88, 93; gender-role attitude, 50; major role of, 109-10, 133; negative perceptions of, 8, 13 n.23, 118, 133; occupational background, 88, 133; party affiliation, 88; pattern of career development, 88-91; recruitment, 13 n.23, 88-89, 133; regional background, 88; table of, 65. *See also* proportional representation party list system; sample; women legislators

Aquino, Corazon, 15, 135, 140 n.12

Aquino, Benigno, 140 n.8

Asia, 87

assassination, 8, 14 n.26, 16, 91

Assemblywomen. *See* women legislators

assertiveness, 128

authoritarianism, 71. *See also* political culture

autonomy, 110; lack of, 110

Bandaranaike, Sirimavo, 1, 12